CALDERÓN

LIFE IS A DREAM

CALDERÓN

LIFE IS A DREAM

La Vida Es Sueño

TRANSLATION AND INTRODUCTION

BY WILLIAM E. COLFORD

BARRON'S EDUCATIONAL SERIES, INC.

New York • London • Toronto • Sydney

INTRODUCTION

1. THE PERIOD

If a student of Comparative Literature or of the Humanities were asked how he would choose the most representative play in a nation's dramatic literature he would say, in all probability, "I would read the masterwork of the master craftsman of the Golden Age in their theater." In Spain this could mean only one thing: *La vida es sueño,* by Calderón. No single play in the Spanish language has enjoyed such an international reputation for more than three centuries; no single play is so universally esteemed and quoted throughout the Hispanic world, on both sides of the Atlantic, as this masterpiece by the last of the great dramatists of Spain's Golden Age.

To classify Calderón's *La vida es sueño* as his finest achievement is high praise indeed, for he composed over two hundred works for the stage, many of them among the best in the national theater; but to assign this play first place in a country where there was an astonishing number of master playwrights during Calderón's lifetime is to appreciate the position held in Spanish letters by this profound philosophical drama. Only *Hamlet* and *Faust* can be compared with it in their respective literatures. And when we consider that Calderón composed his masterwork in his early thirties, while Shakespeare's great drama was produced at the peak of his artistic maturity and Goethe's classic was the result of lifelong endeavors, we begin to realize still more the merits of the Spanish author, who gave up writing secular plays and entered the priesthood at an age when men of letters are approaching the prime of their creative powers. His abilities were then turned to the writing of religious plays called *autos sacra-mentales*—his "starry *autos*," to use Shelley's term. Calderón's works in this genre are unsurpassed in Spanish literature. That the theme "life is a dream" was deep-rooted in the author's heart and mind is revealed by the fact that one of these *autos* is an allegorical version of the same subject and bears the same title as the secular drama written forty years earlier: *La vida es sueño*.

Calderón's long life (1600-1681) almost completely encompasses the reigns of the last three Hapsburg kings of Spain: Philip III (1598-1621), Philip IV (1621-1665), and Charles II (1665-1700). In the seventeenth century the sun had already begun to set on the Spanish Empire; but twilight is often the most beautiful time of day. The golden glow of this cultural twilight shone with particular brilliance on the Court of Philip IV, patron of the arts and of men of letters, including Calderón. The high point of Spanish classical literature coincided with the flowering of the Spanish school of painting. El Greco's gaunt, mystic figures were still contemporary art, for he died when Calderón was a youth (1614). Ribera (1588-1656) and Zurbarán (1598-1662) were producing their magnificent canvasses, and the official Court painter, Velázquez (1599-1660), based one of his most famous compositions, "The Surrender of Breda" (*Las lanzas*), on a vivid scene in Calderón's play *El sitio de Breda*. Murillo (1617-1682) outlived Calderón by one year; the death of these two closes the Golden Age of Spanish culture.

In the field of letters Cervantes, who died in 1616, dominated the novel during Calderón's early youth. But as the century wore on, and gold from the New World passed through Spain to the bankers in Italy and Northern Europe, leaving inflation and corruption in its wake, the growing economic and moral crisis cast lengthening shadows over the nation. The seamy side of life in Spain came to the fore in the exaggerated naturalism of the picaresque novel, widely imitated throughout Europe. This trend toward deep pessimism and disillusionment is exemplified in the satirical works of Quevedo, in prose and in verse, which kept pouring from his prolific pen until his death in 1645.

In poetry, the style of Góngora (1561-1627) came to affect most subsequent verse, lyric and dramatic, during the rest of the seventeenth century. Calderón, who began to write his plays when the triumph of gongorism was complete, is not free from the obscurities of this style (also called *culteranismo*) although the subtleties of the parallel literary movement called *conceptismo* are more prevalent in his works. A word of explanation is in order.

Briefly, *culteranismo* was the ostentation of "culture": an affected erudition calculated to lend artificial brilliance to literary style by the excessive use of classical allusions and mythological references; extravagant metaphors and strained imagery; the use of archaic words, and the introduction of neologisms, or the use of standard words with deliberately obscure meanings; and a strongly latinized syntax which often did violence to the Spanish language by the suppression of articles and conjunctions, the twisting of the word order, and the abuse of rhetorical devices. It was, in effect, another manifestation of the aesthetic crisis of seventeenth-century Spain, the literary counterpart of the architectural and decorative extravagances of the baroque and the churrigueresque. Góngora's *Polifemo* and *Las soledades* are the two most celebrated poems in this "manner." Spain was not alone in this literary phenomenon, which was called euphuism in England, *préciosité* in France and *marinismo* in Italy.

Conceptismo, on the other hand, manifested itself mainly in prose. It consisted of ultra-refined subtleties in ideas, and clever playing with the meanings of words: a sort of semantic symbolism. The chief exponents of this style were Quevedo and the Jesuit philosopher Baltasar Gracián. Calderón, whose agile mind had been trained in logic, law, and theology at the University of Salamanca, leans more toward *conceptismo* than toward *culteranismo*. Moreover, a lyric poet might pen his obscure gongoristic verses for a small inner circle of initiates, but a dramatic poet had to reach the public and be understood. Hence, Calderón avoids the extremes of both movements, although some passages in his plays are studded with extravagant images and relatively obscure meanings. *La vida es sueño* is comparatively free of these, however.

In the field of drama itself, the age of Calderón produced Spain's mightiest figures. Lope de Vega (1562-1635) is, after Cervantes, the greatest creative genius in Spanish letters. He gave order and new luster to the scattered earlier efforts, and enriched dramatic doctrine to the extent that in the literary history of Spain it is customary to speak of the theater "before Lope" or "after Lope." He is the founder of the modern drama written in the Spanish language: basically realistic, yet highly romantic in its rejection of all classical rules and in its complete freedom of expression for the playwright's fancy.

Lope was the most popular idol of his day (even more so than Cervantes), and amassed a fortune from his literary works. The possessor of the most fertile imagination and the most facile pen in the history of the theater, he wrote more than 1,500 plays. His was a rich vein which yielded some of the purest ore of the Golden Age, for example, *Peribáñez, Fuenteovejuna, El mejor alcalde, el rey,* and *La estrella de Sevilla.* But such a copious production was bound to be uneven, and his work is broad rather than deep. He is a brilliant and exciting painter of the Spanish scene, but not a philosopher or interpreter of his times. Calderón, whose work as a young dramatist won fulsome praise from Lope, is clearly the better craftsman.

There were still other giants of the Spanish theater during Calderón's day. After Don Quixote, Spain's most renowned fictional character is the impious libertine Don Juan, one of the greatest figures in world literature. He was created by a priest, Father Gabriel Téllez, better known by his pen name of Tirso de Molina (1584-1639). Tirso, second only to Lope in fecundity, wrote more than four hundred plays; but the one called *El burlador de Sevilla* (1630) gave to the world the dramatic Don Juan, who has inspired men of such diverse talents as Molière, Mozart, Byron, Zorrilla, Dumas, G. B. Shaw and Richard Strauss.

We must mention also dramatists of such stature as Alarcón (1581-1639), the Mexican-born hunchback who is the great moralist of the Spanish theater (*Las paredes oyen, La verdad sospechosa*) and an impeccable stylist. And then there is Guillén de Castro (1569-1630), the noble and dashing cavalry captain who brought to life in his plays the heroic deeds of the Middle Ages. His masterpiece is *Las mocedades del Cid,* upon which Corneille based his classic *Le Cid.* Other outstanding playwrights formed a veritable galaxy of stars during the time of Calderón: Pérez de Montalbán (1602-1638), who wrote the traditional *Los amantes de Teruel,* based on the same theme as the Romantic play of the same name by the nineteenth-century Spanish critic Juan Eugenio Hartzenbusch, whose edition of *La vida es sueño* was published in the monumental Biblioteca de Autores Españoles; Rojas Zorrilla (1607-1648), author of the tragic honor play *Del rey abajo, ninguno;* and Agustín Moreto (1618-1669), Calderón's only serious rival during his later years, who wrote the splendid character study *El desdén con el desdén.*

The list would be almost endless. The Spaniards were considered the masters of the theater in seventeenth-century Europe, and their plays were freely "borrowed" or rewritten, particulary by the French. One interesting detail shows the growing centralization of Spanish culture in Madrid during Calderón's day: the overwhelming majority of the most outstanding authors of the Golden Age, particularly the playwrights, were natives of Madrid, including Quevedo, Lope de Vega, Tirso de Molina, Pérez de Montalbán, Agustín Moreto, and Calderón himself. That *La vida es sueño* should be considered the most representative single play (although Don Juan is the most renowned single character) among the many masterpieces of the seventeenth-century Spanish theater is due to qualities we shall discuss after a brief examination of the life and other works of Calderón.

2. THE AUTHOR

Don Pedro Calderón de la Barca came from a highly respected Madrid family. His father, an accountant in the Royal Treasury, died when the boy was fifteen; Pedro's mother had died five years earlier. But the estate was ample, coupled with the favor of a rich grandmother, to provide for Pedro and his older brother Diego, his younger brother José, and his sister Dorotea, who later became a nun. He was educated at a Jesuit school in Madrid, and subsequently at the University of Alcalá not far from that city. After a year he transferred to the University of Salamanca, where he took his degree in canonical law in 1619.

Pedro could have practiced law, or entered the Church by taking up an endowed family chaplaincy, but like many young Spanish noblemen of the time his preference was for arms, both military and feminine. An accomplished swordsman, he was involved in many duels and numerous escapades, and was even wounded during a dispute over a theatrical rehearsal! After gallant service with the army in Italy and in Flanders, Calderón returned to Spain and became a courtier at Madrid. His skill in writing and directing plays won him the favor of Philip IV, whose official Court entertainer he became, just as his contemporary, Molière, was at Versailles for Louis XIV a few years later. His handsome, intellectual appearance, his wit and brilliant conversational ability attracted much attention. In 1637 the king granted him the much-coveted habit of a Knight of Santiago, and he continued to receive high honors at Court all his long life. Calderón was always greatly respected personally, and was not involved in the bitter polemics so prevalent in seventeenth-century literary circles.

A little-stressed facet of his early theatrical endeavors is his production of light plays with music, singing, and dancing: he was the originator of the famous "zarzuelas," Spain's delightful type of modern musical comedy. The name stems from the fact that Calderón produced them originally at King Philip's hunting lodge, "La Zarzuela," outside the capital.

In addition to composing these lighter works, he won several prizes for lyric poetry at the contests held in honor of the patron of Madrid, Saint Isidore. And from Lope he earned the compliment that he had "gained in youth the laurels that time usually reserves for gray hairs." We know also from Montalbán that in the early 1630's (the period of *La vida es sueño*) Calderón's plays were being presented in Madrid with great success. The years

1630 to 1650 mark the high point of his activity in the field of the drama.

In 1650 Calderón stopped writing for public presentation (although he continued to supervise some palace spectacles), and took holy orders. He had been saddened by the loss of his two brothers (Diego was killed in a duel and José was killed in action with the army), and by the death of his mistress, who had borne him a son. He went first to Toledo, but was recalled and made private chaplain to King Philip IV. For the next thirty years Calderón produced two *autos sacramentales* each year for the municipality of Madrid. When he died in 1681 all Spain mourned, and his funeral was a national affair. With him, the Golden Age of Spanish literature passed away.

Several times Calderón's *autos* have been mentioned. The *auto sacramental* developed out of the religious plays of the Middle Ages, and took on new elaborateness after Pope Urban IV instituted the Feast of the Most Blessed Sacrament in 1264. To this day, the Corpus Christi celebrations are much more colorful in Hispanic countries than elsewhere. In Calderón's time this was the biggest religious festival of the year. There were outdoor processions, and religious spectacles on floats in commemoration of the Eucharist. The *auto* had evolved as a distinct dramatic form about 1500. Lope developed it to new heights, but it was Calderón who brought it to such a peak of perfection that the term became virtually synonymous with his name. His death left a great void in the Spanish theater, since no one replaced him; but his *autos sacramentales* were performed as standard repertoire until the second half of the eighteenth century, when the pro-Encyclopedist King Charles III forbade the spectacles as contrary to good taste.

The *auto sacramental* was a one-act allegorical play, usually on a Biblical or other sacred theme (although some of them used widely diversified subjects), performed in the public squares of the towns of Spain and Spanish America after the siesta on Corpus Christi day. Ingeniously contrived floats were grouped about a platform, and the actors passed from one to the other as the action of the play demanded. There was much rivalry among the towns and cities to produce the best *autos,* but naturally Madrid's were most elaborate. Some of Calderón's finest flights of lyric poetry are to be found in these religious works. A good example of this type of allegory is the *auto* he wrote on the theme of *La vida es sueño.* In this version the characters of the secular drama have been turned into abstractions such as Man, Wisdom, Free Will, Grace, Love, etc. Segismundo's triumph over himself is likened to the redemption of fallen man through the Sacraments of Baptism and Communion (Corpus Christi).

Although Calderón cultivated every kind of theatrical production known in his day, including musicals, farces, historical plays, "honor" tragedies, and full-length theological dramas, he excelled in three major types: the *auto sacramental* described above, the "cloak-and-sword" comedy, and the philosophical drama, of which *La vida es sueño* is his masterpiece.

The famous *comedias de capa y espada,* so called because of the sweeping cloak and ready sword so typical of the Spanish gallant of the seventeenth century, were highly popular, and Calderón is rightly considered the master of this genre. These *comedias* (and it should be recalled that any secular play, regardless of its subject or outcome, was called a *comedia*) were essentially melodramatic in nature, with love and honor the central themes. The situations are extremely complicated, with muffled *caballeros* and veiled *señoritas* involved in amorous intrigues: secret hiding places, double doors, jealous lovers, and much flashing swordplay. A man caught duelling was subject to punishment by the civil authorities, of course; and if he died without absolution for a sin committed in connection with the duel, the ecclesiastical authorities condemned him to eternal damnation. Hence, a man who risked not only his life but also his immortal soul in order to keep his honor clean was considered a truly heroic figure. Written by an expert swordman for an audience full of duelists, the impact of these plays was tremendous. Calderón captures the customs of the times in these period pieces, and shows masterly skill in weaving the intricate plots. Many of them follow a well-established formula; Goethe, who admired Calderón's works greatly, once remarked that these cloak-and-sword plays were "as like as bullets." It is the surprise solution of a love or honor dilemma that holds the audience captive to the last line. The titles of two of Calderón's best in this genre reveal the nature of the plays: *Casa con dos puertas mala es de guardar* and *El escondido y la tapada.*

"Calderonian honor" is an expression that has passed into the Spanish language as indicative of a relentless, implacable sense of duty to a rigid code of behavior. The Spanish concept of honor had been treated effectively by Lope and his followers, but it remained for Calderón to capture it for all time on the seventeenth-century stage. The many ramifications of the code involved the relationships between a subject and his king, among nobles, and especially toward women, married and unmarried. These customs were a composite of medieval chivalry and Moorish usages, which resulted in a severity that seems excessive from the modern viewpoint. Jealousy, almost always unfounded, and righteous revenge for real wrongs, are the chief themes of these gripping tragedies. Blood was the only cleansing solution that would remove the stain of an affront, real or fancied. This was particularly true in questions involving even the slightest breath of suspicion of marital infidelity. Calderón wrote several of these gory tragedies of jealousy, in which the sympathy of the audience is directed toward the Othellos rather than the Desdemonas, not so much by the author as by the prevailing code of honor. The best are *El médico de su honra* and *A secreto agravio, secreta venganza*.

Another typical honor situation is portrayed in the rustic masterpiece *El alcalde de Zalamea*. Lope had written a drama based on the same tradition, and with the same title. His is a good play, but only that; Calderón's is the most perfect piece of Spanish stagecraft in this genre. It is a good illustration of the manner in which Calderón inherited all the great traditions and accumulated lore of the Spanish theater, and then with his own spark of genius brought the Golden Age of drama to its peak of perfection.

Pedro Crespo, a humble, law-abiding farmer who is unanimously chosen mayor of Zalamea, is dishonored when an arrogant captain temporarily quartered in his house seduces and abandons his daughter. Instead of killing the king's officer on the spot, Mayor Crespo arrests him and performs the marriage ceremony; then he hangs the captain just as King Philip II arives. With great respect toward his monarch, yet reserving to himself the democratic prerogatives always retained by the Spanish people, Pedro Crespo explains that in questions of honor like this, only he himself can be the judge. The king, impressed by the great personal dignity of the farmer-mayor, and in agreement with his stern code of justice, grants him the royal pardon. Many critics consider this the most polished work of the Spanish classic theater. Certainly Calderón has given us here an unforgettable gallery of literary portraits, together with some passages of his best dramatic verse.

As a final example of Calderón's work in other types of drama—and all the elements we have been delineating are necessary for a full understanding of *La vida es sueño*—we should cite the theological play *El mágico prodigioso.* It is based on the legend of Cyprian of Antioch, who, tormented by doubts, renounces science and theology in order to gain possession of a lovely maiden by means of magic arts and a soul-selling pact with the Devil. (The play so interested Shelley, who considered Calderón the European dramatist *par excellence,* that he translated it into English.) In the Spanish treatment of this Faustian theme, the girl—Justina—resists all temptation through her deep faith. Cyprian, converted to Christianity, suffered martyrdom at her side, and both were canonized by the Church. The theological and metaphysical discussions between Cyprian and the Devil place this work in a double religious-philosophical category. It is this element of dialectics that appealed to Calderón's subtle mind, and which is so evident in many of his plays. This is especially true in *La vida es sueño,* which combines elements of the honor tragedy and the theological drama to form his philosophical masterpiece.

3. THE WORK

The basic theme of Prince Segismundo's imprisonment by King Basilio in *La vida es sueño* may be traced to Oriental sources. The first is the tale of Barlaam and Josephat, in which an Indian potentate, a bitter enemy of Christianity, hears the wisest of his astrologers predict that his new-born son Josephat will become a Christian. To prevent this the king secludes the boy in the mountain fastnesses, but Barlaam, a holy hermit, seeks him out and converts him to the new faith. If Calderón did not know of the original source of the story, which was a favorite of medieval Europe, he might have read Lope's account of it in *Los dos soldados de Cristo,* or *Barlán y Josafá.* Also, he might have derived some small part of the idea from Lope's play *El hijo de Reduán,* in which a Moorish prince is brought up by rough shepherds until his return to the palace where he reacts violently.

The second Oriental element is the drugging of Segismundo and his enjoyment of one glorious day of power; it is found in the *Arabian Nights.* The Caliph Haroun al Raschid had an opiate given to his companion Abou Hassan, who awakened in the palace and enjoyed royal prerogatives for a day. Then he was drugged again and taken home; upon awakening he thought it had all been a dream. This theme of the "awakened sleeper" found its way to the West, too. The Caliph became Philp the Good, Duke of Burgundy (1396-1467), and Hassan became in the Occidental version a drunken beggar who was regaled for a day and returned to the gutter. Variants of the same theme are found in Boccacio's *Decameron* and in Shakespeare's Induction to *The Taming of the Shrew.* The nearest source during Calderón's formative years was a popular play by Agustín de Rojas (1572-1618) called *El viaje entretenido,* in which the locale is transferred to Spain. By merging these two Oriental tales, adding the "honor" element in the sub-plot of Rosaura and Astolfo, and infusing the whole with Catholic orthodoxy, Calderón produced a work truly representative of the seventeenth-century Spanish spirit. This Orientalism is perhaps what inspired James Russell Lowell, in his poem *The Nightingale in the Study,* to call him

> *My Calderón, my nightingale,*
> *My Arab soul in Spanish feathers.*

Criticism has been levelled at Calderón for his introduction of the secondary intrigue involving the affair of honor which caused such anguish in Clotaldo, who was torn between the need to avenge the affront to his long-lost daughter and his loyalty to the code of vassalage. Actually, this is done with such skill that it becomes part and parcel of the whole drama, just as Shakespeare interweaves the Gloucester-Edgar-Edmund story with the Lear legend to form his classic tragedy of old age. Basilio, however, is not the central figure, nor is he, like Lear, "every inch a king."

It is Segismundo who dominates the drama, just as Pedro Crespo does in *El alcalde de Zalamea* and Cipriano does in *El mágico prodigioso.* This stress upon the protagonist differentiates Calderón from Lope, and gives great emphasis to the dramatic monologue. Segismundo's curtain speech at the end of Act II is to the Spanish stage what Hamlet's immortal soliloquy is to the Elizabethan theater: the most famous passage in the literature. And the Prince of Denmark, too, is concerned about what it is

> To sleep: perchance to dream . . .

In addition to emphasizing the individual hero in his dramas, Calderón stresses the ideological element. In *La vida es sueño* it is the basic conflict between free will and predestination, i.e., whether Segismundo can triumph over the fate predicted for him. Calderón's solution lies clearly within the framework of orthodox Catholicism: this life has meaning only in terms of the life everlasting. Segismundo, captive in his cave, is the symbol of mankind held in the prison of spiritual darkness. The whole problem is to free himself from the chains that bind him to his earthly instincts and to earn eternal salvation through faith and good works. This he does through self-discipline: he pardons his erstwhile enemies, and then settles Clotaldo's honor conflict by ordering Astolfo to marry Rosaura. Segismundo's own marriage to Estrella is typical of the rapid solution of many love and honor dilemmas in the last scene of Spanish classic plays. The unexpected death of the stock Spanish comic Clarín adds a tragic touch and an additional moral lesson to the drama.

The fact that the action takes place in Poland and not in Spain has no special significance, except perhaps to add a long-ago-and-far-away element to the play as presented to seventeenth-century Spanish audiences, just as we today might locate a plot like this in Graustark or Ruritania to strike an exotic note and at the same time to emphasize the universal message of the theme.

Calderón's stress upon the individual hero like Segismundo, the spiritual restlessness of his protagonists torn by inner doubts, and the religious element in his metaphysical dramas, endeared him to the Romantics of the nineteenth century. Not only did Goethe and Shelley place Calderón in the forefront of the world's great dramatists, but the Schlegel brothers, leading German literary critics of that period, saw in him the highest peak of the whole Golden Age in Spain. As a matter of fact, the Spanish public had never ceased to love Calderón all during the neoclassic eighteenth century; and the cult of Calderón, whose theater was inherently anti-classical, led to the flowering of the Romantic drama in nineteenth-century Spain.

Although modern literary criticism has tended to redress the balance and place Lope the fertile creator above Calderón the thoughtful artist, for the Spanish people themselves Calderón remains the national dramatist. No other playwright sums up so well that "tragic sense of life" (Unamuno's phrase) which is present to such an eminent degree in the Spanish spirit: the assurance of individual worth and the deep personal dignity visible in the profile of the poorest peasant; the mask of suffering on the expressive face of a "flamenco" dancer; the haunting Moorish overtones of the Spanish guitar; the Senecan stoicism of the *torero* as the rapid rhythm and melancholy minor strain of the *pasodoble* summon him to the ritual dance of death that is the bullfight. All this deeply Spanish spirit Calderón has captured in his works. And his masterpiece, *La vida es sueño,* combines the religious orthodoxy of seventeenth-century Spain, spearhead of the Counter-Reformation, with a universal note that makes it one of the great works of world literature.

4. THE TRANSLATION

La vida es sueño has thus far been adapted or translated into Dutch, English, French, German, Italian, and Russian. Edward FitzGerald, whose quatrains of Omar Khayyam won such fame in the nineteenth century, freely adapted *La vida es sueño* into a play to which he gave the Shakespearean title *Such stuff as dreams are made of.* There have been other versions in the twentieth century for the English stage and for the British Broadcasting Corporation. The most frequently used verse translation, found in anthologies of world drama, is the one by Denis F. MacCarthy done in London in 1873. It has some fine passages, but unfortunately forces the translation to follow the fluctuating patterns of the Spanish meter. This Procrustean technique often results in violence to the English. A translation into prose and verse done by the Englishman William Stirling in Havana in 1942 is far better, but evidently was a very limited edition; there is only one catalogued copy in the United States, in the Hispanic section of the Library of Congress. This present volume, then, is intended to present for the first time to the American student of Comparative Literature a complete verse translation into the meter of the Elizabethan dramatists, iambic pentameters.

Spanish dramatic verse established no norms of its own, such as the alexandrine of the French classic theater; it simply adopted the many meters already in use by the lyric poets. In this play Calderón employs six different metrical arrangements with great technical skill: *romances, silvas, redondillas, octavas, quintillas,* and *décimas.* Of these, the *romance* predominates. This, the measure of the old Spanish ballads, is the national verse-form, and was one factor in determining the use of our standard verse-form in the translation. There is no similarity between them beyond this national note, for the whole system of Spanish prosody is antithetical to the English: syllables are counted instead of feet. The eight-syllable *romance* forms a short line of verse compared to the iambic pentameters of the Elizabethan theater; therefore, two of Calderón's lines often combine into one line of translation, which makes the English version seem shorter than the Spanish was in the original play.

Sometimes Calderón's diction is extremely simple for such a profound drama; the English has tried to reflect this faithfully. At other times, his *culteranismo* and his *conceptismo* are quite obscure even in the original language; moreover, some of his seventeenth-century "conceits" and plays on words would mean nothing in strict translation. Therefore, the present version has tried to present these elements to the reader by conveying to the English-speaking mind what the original conveyed to the Spanish-speaking mind, and by rendering not a too-slavish literal translation nor a too-free literary translation, but one that strikes a balance between the two: what we might call a "literate" translation.

New York, 1957 W. E. C.

BIBLIOGRAPHY

SOME READILY AVAILABLE EDITIONS IN SPANISH

P. Calderón de la Barca: Teatro, Biblioteca de Autores Españoles, vols. VII, IX, XII, XIV.

Obras completas, Madrid, 1932, 1947 (2 vols.).

La vida es sueño, ed. Comfort, New York, 1904.

Three plays, ed. Northup, Boston, 1926.

La vida es sueño: comedia famosa y auto sacramental, Santiago de Chile, 1955. (A good, inexpensive edition for comparing the play with the *auto*).

STUDIES: GENERAL

H. A. Rennert, *The Spanish stage in the time of Lope de Vega,* New York, 1909.

L.-P. Thomas, *Le lyrisme et la préciosité cultistes en Espagne,* Halle, 1909.

E. K. Kane, *Gongorism and the Golden Age,* Chapel Hill, N. C., 1928.

K. Vossler, *Lope de Vega y su tiempo,* Madrid, 1932.

G. T. Northup, *An introduction to Spanish literature*, Chicago, 1936.

A. del Río, *Historia de la literatura española*, New York, 1948.

M. Romera Navarro, *Historia de la literatura española*, Boston, 1949.

STUDIES: SPECIFIC

M. Menéndez y Pelayo, *Calderón y su teatro*, Madrid, 1881.

A. Farinelli, *La vita è un sogno*, Turin, 1916 (2 vols.). (Contains a study of the dream motif in world literature.)

E. Cotarelo, *Ensayo sobre la vida y obras de Don Pedro Calderón de la Barca*, Madrid, 1924.

L. E. Weir, *The ideas embodied in the religious drama of Calderón*, Lincoln, Neb., 1940.

A. Parker, *The allegorical drama of Calderón*, London, 1943.

TRANSLATIONS INTO ENGLISH: GENERAL

A. Flores, *Spanish literature in English translation: a bibliographical syllabus*, New York, 1926.

R. U. Pane, *English translations from the Spanish, 1484-1943*, New Brunswick, N. J., 1944.

TRANSLATIONS INTO ENGLISH: SPECIFIC

R. C. Trend, *Calderón, his life and genius, with specimens of his plays*, London, 1856.

D. F. MacCarthy, *Life is a dream*, London, 1873.

E. FitzGerald, *Eight dramas of Calderón, freely translated*, London, 1906.

F. Birch and J. B. Trend, *Life's a dream, translated for the English stage*, Cambridge, England, 1925.

C. Morgan, *Life's a dream*, BBC Great Plays Booklet No. 4, London, 1928.
W. F. Stirling, *Life is a dream*, Havana, 1942.

DRAMATIS PERSONAE

BASILIO: King of Poland

SEGISMUNDO: Prince, and son to Basilio

ASTOLFO: Duke of Muscovy, nephew to Basilio

CLOTALDO: Old tutor of Segismundo

CLARÍN: Comic servant of Rosaura

ESTRELLA: Princess, niece to Basilio

ROSAURA: Daughter to Clotaldo

Soldiers, Guards, Musicians, Servants, Ladies, Attendants

————————

*The action takes place at the Court of Poland, in a
fortress nearby, and in the open country.*

setting: Poland

ACT ONE

At one side a rugged mountain, and at the other a tower whose ground floor serves as a prison for SEGISMUNDO. *The door, which faces the audience, is partially open. Night is falling as the action begins.*

SCENE ONE

ROSAURA, *dressed as a man, appears on the rocky height, and comes down to level ground;* CLARÍN *follows her.*

ROSAURA: Wild hippogriff,[1] that matched the wind in flight,
            Dark lightning, dull-plumed bird, unscalèd fish,
            Brute beast that makes a mock of nature's laws,
            Now wherefore art thou come in headlong plunge
            Through twisting trails to reach this barren brink?
            Remain upon this crag so beasts may have
            Their Phaëthon;[2] for I, with no more course
            Than destiny decrees, in blind despair
            Descend the tangled slope of this harsh hill
            That wrinkles to the sun its scowling brow.
            A poor reception, Poland, dost thou give
            A stranger, since with blood her welcome's writ
            Upon thy sands, and hardly here, she fares

---

[1] Hippogriff: *a fabulous creature, half horse and half griffin (Ariosto,* Orlando furioso). *This opening speech by Rosaura is an example of* culteranismo.
[2] Phaëthon: *son of Helios. He drove the chariot of the sun too near the earth, which he almost set on fire.*

I

So hardly. Yet my fate ordains it so.
But where was pity e'er found for one in woe?

CLARÍN: Say two in woe: include me in thy plaint.
For if as two we left our land in search
Of fame, and then as two came here through mad
Misfortune, and as two fell down this slope,
Should I not merit mention for my pains?

ROSAURA: I do not mention thee in my lament,
Clarín, lest thus in weeping for thy cares
I take away thy right to be consoled.
For sighing's such delight, a wise man thought,
That for this pleasure trouble should be sought.

CLARÍN: That sage was just a graybeard in his cups.
If only he'd received a thousand whacks
He could have wept for joy at such a gift!
But what, my lady, shall we do afoot,
Alone, astray, and at this hour upon
A barren hill as sunlight starts to fade?

ROSAURA: Whoever saw such strange events! But if
My eyes are not deceived by fancy's flight,
They glimpse a building by day's paling light.

CLARÍN: Unless my longing lies, I see its shape.

ROSAURA: A country palace rises 'mid bare hills,
So small it shrinks to look up at the sun.
Its form and size are such that at the foot
Of sun-tipped crags and cliffs all circling 'round
It's like a boulder toppled to the ground.

CLARÍN: Let us draw near, my lady; we have looked
Enough; 'twere better that those kindly folk
Should let us in.

Clarin to accompany Rosaura to her exile
He complains a lot.

ROSAURA: The door (or rather say
                    A ghastly cave) is open, and its womb
                    Gives birth to night, engendered in that gloom.
                              [*Chains clank within*]
CLARÍN: What is that sound I hear, by Heaven's will!
ROSAURA: I stand transfixed, a mass of fire and chill!
CLARÍN: Is that the clanking of a chain I hear?
                    Upon my life! Some convict's ghost, I fear.

SCENE TWO

                    Segismundo, inside the tower; Rosaura, Clarín.

SEGISMUNDO: [*Within*] Oh, wretched me! Alas, unhappy man!
ROSAURA: What doleful voice is that I overhear?
                    New pains and torments I must start to fight.
CLARÍN: And I begin to struggle with new fright.
ROSAURA: Clarín!
CLARÍN: My lady?
ROSAURA: Let us turn and fly
                    The dangers of this haunted tow'r.
CLARÍN: But I
                    Do not have strength to run, or even try!
ROSAURA: Is not that scanty glow some dying breath,
                    A pallid star that in faint flickerings,
                    In throbbing ardors, palpitating rays,
                    Makes darker that dim room with doubtful light?
                    Why, yes! By its reflection I can see
                    (Though from afar) a gloomy prison that
                    Unto a living dead man is a tomb;
                    And even more surprising to me still,
                    In bestial clothing lies a man in chains,

With just a lamp for company. But since
We cannot flee, from this spot let us hear
His troubles, and to what he says give ear.

[*The door opens fully, revealing* SEGISMUNDO *in chains, and
dressed in animal skins. A light shines within the tower.*]

SEGISMUNDO: Oh, wretched me! Alas, unhappy man!
I strive, oh Heav'n, since I am treated so,
To find out what my crime against thee was
In being born; although in being born
I understand just what my crime has been.
Thy judgment harsh has had just origin:
To have been born is mankind's greatest sin.
I only seek to know, to ease my grief,
(Now setting to one side the crime of birth)
In what way greater, Heav'n, could I offend,
To merit from thee greater punishment?
Were not all others born? If so, in fine,
What dispensation theirs that was not mine?
Birds are born, rich garbed in hues that give
Them brilliant beauty; then, when scarcely more
Than feathered flow'rs or plumèd garlands, breast
The vault of air with speedy wing, and leave
The shelt'ring nest forlorn. And what of me?
Should I, with soul much greater, be less free?
Beasts are born, their skin all mottled o'er
With lovely colors; then, when scarcely more
Than starry patches, limned with learnèd brush,
The needs of man instruct them to be bold,

Cruel monsters in their lair. And what of me?
Should I, with higher instincts, be less free?
Fish are born, unbreathing spawn of ooze
And slimy seaweed; then, when scarcely more
Than tiny boats with scales upon the waves,
They swim away to measure all the vast
Cold limits of the deep. And what of me?
Should I, with greater free will, be less free?
Streams are born, and serpent-like uncoil
Among the flow'rs; then, when scarcely more
Than silv'ry snakes, they wind away and sing
In tuneful praise the rustic majesty
Stretched open to their flight. And what of me?
Should I, with life much longer, be less free?
And as I reach this angry pitch I burn
With Etna's[3] fierce volcanic fires, and want
To tear my heart in pieces from my breast.
What law, what reason can deny to man
That gift so sweet, so natural, that God
Has giv'n a stream, a fish, a beast, a bird?

ROSAURA: Fear and pity are instilled in me
            By his opinions.

SEGISMUNDO: Who has heard my cries?
            Is that you, Clotaldo?

CLARÍN: [Aside to his lady.] Tell him yes.

ROSAURA: It's only one forlorn (oh, woe is me!)
            Who in these frigid vaults o'erheard thy plea.

―――――――――――――
[3] Etna: *volcanic mountain in northeast Sicily.*

SEGISMUNDO: Then I must kill thee here in order that

                                  [*Seizing her*]

         Thou may'st not know—for I know thou dost know—
         My weakness. Just because thou heardest me,
         With these strong arms I must tear thee to bits.

CLARÍN (coward): I am deaf, and could not overhear!

ROSAURA: If thou art human, let my prostrate form
         Before thy feet suffice to set me free.

SEGISMUNDO: Thy voice has moved me, thy appearance stays
a voice make me less angry   My hand, and the respect I feel for thee
         Disturbs me. Who art thou? Although in here
         I know so little of the world, because
live his life in the cave   This tow'r has been my cradle and my tomb;
         And though since birth (if this is what birth is)
         I only know this desert region where
         I'm living like a living skeleton,
         A dead man who's alive; and though I've seen
         And talked to just one person here who feels
         Compassion for my sorrows, and through whom
         I have some notion of Heav'n and earth;
         And though thou may'st be more amazed and call
         Me human monster in thy stunned surprise,
         I am a man among wild beasts, a wild
         Beast among men; and though amid such grave
         Misfortunes I have studied politics,
         Informed by animals and taught by birds,
         And I have traced the paths of pallid stars;
         'Tis thou alone hast brought such passion to
         My anger, admiration to my eyes,
         And wonder to my ears. Each time I see

Thee I am more amazed, and when I look
Upon thee more, still more I want to look.
I think my eyes must have the dropsy, for
When drinking's death, they drink thee in the more;
And so, while seeing that seeing means death
To me, I am dying to see. But let
Me look at thee and die, for I know not,
Though seeing you means death, what not to see
Might mean. It would be worse than savage death,
Than fury, wrath, and deepest grief: it would
Be life; thus I have learned its bitterness,
For giving life to one importunate ,
Is giving death to one that's fortunate.

ROSAURA:

she is astounded

I look at thee with wonder, and I hear
Thee with astonishment, and do not know
What I can say to thee, nor what to ask.
I'll only say that to this place today
Heaven has guided me to be consoled,
If it can be the consolation of
A wretch to see one who's more wretched still.
The tale is told about a wise man who
One day—so poor and destitute was he—
Had only lived upon some herbs he picked;
"Can there be another man," he said

feeling sorry for himself

Within himself, "who's poorer and unhappier
Than I?" And when he turned his head he found
The answer as he saw another sage
Was picking up the leaves he threw away.
Complaining of my lot I went along
Existing in this world, and just when I

Rosaura realizes it is better to be in exile rather than in chains.

Was saying to myself, "Is there a soul
Alive whose lot is more unfortunate?",
Thou mercifully didst the answer give
To me; for just as in the fable, I
Discover that my woes—in order to
Convert them into joys—thou hast picked up.
And if perchance my woes can be of some
Relief to thee, please pay me careful heed,
And help thyself to those I do not need.
I am . . .

SCENE THREE

CLOTALDO, SOLDIERS, SEGISMUNDO, ROSAURA, CLARÍN.

CLOTALDO: [*Within*] Ho! Tower guards! Asleep or craven,
            You have allowed two persons to break in
            This jail!

ROSAURA: I am again confused.

SEGISMUNDO: It is
            Clotaldo; he's my jailer. Are my woes
            Not ended yet?

CLOTALDO: [*Within*] Come on, and look alive!
            Before they can defend themselves, seize them
            Or kill them!

VOICES FROM WITHIN: Treason!

CLARÍN: Tower guards,
            Who let us come in here, since you give us
            A choice, to seize us is much easier.

    [CLOTALDO *and the soldiers come out; he is carrying a pistol, and all have their faces covered.*]

CLOTALDO: [*Aside to the soldiers as they appear*]
Let everybody cover up his face;
It is important to be cautious and
Let no one recognize us in this place.

CLARÍN: And so we have a little masquerade?

CLOTALDO: Oh, you unknowing people who the bounds
And limits of this place forbidd'n have passed
Against the king's decree, which orders that
No person dare set eyes upon the freak
Of nature hid among these rocks, lay down
Your weapons and give up, or else this gun,
This metal snake, will spew the venom of
Its piercing double sting, whose flash will rend
The air.

SEGISMUNDO: Before, oh tyrant master, thou
Can'st harm or injure them, my life will be
A victim of these wretched chains, for I,
By Heav'n! will tear myself apart in them
With mine own hands or with my teeth within
This cavern, rather than consent to their
Misfortune or bemoan their being abused.

CLOTALDO: If thou dost know that thy misfortunes are
So great, oh Segismundo, that before
Thy birth thou didst, by Heaven's dictum, die;
If thou dost know that this confinement is
A leash to hold thy haughty fury back,
A rein to check it, why then dost thou boast?
[*To the soldiers*] Bolt fast the door of that small cell.
                                        Conceal
Him in there.

Clotaldo will let the King decide

SEGISMUNDO: Oh, Heaven,
How wise thou art in taking liberty
From me! Because I'd be a giant against
Thee, and to break the spheres and crystals of
The sun, upon foundations formed of stone
I'd pile mountains of jasper.

CLOTALDO: Perhaps just so thou may'st not pile them up,
Today thou sufferest so many ills.
[*Some soldiers take* SEGISMUNDO *away and lock
him in his cell.*]

SCENE FOUR

ROSAURA, CLOTALDO, CLARÍN, SOLDIERS.

ROSAURA: Since I have noticed pride offended thee *beg*
So much, I would be foolish not to beg
Thee humbly for this life that lies here at *his life*
Thy feet. May pity move thee, then, in my
Behalf, for it would be severe indeed
If favor were not found in thee by pride
Or by humility.

CLARÍN: And if neither
Humility nor Pride has influence
Upon thee (figures that have acted time
And time again in sacred plays), then I,
Not humble and not proud, but placed somewhere
Between the two extremes, request of thee
That thou come to our aid and set us free.

CLOTALDO: What ho!

SOLDIERS: My lord?

CLOTALDO: From these two take
                    Their weapons, and blindfold their eyes so that
                    They may see neither how nor whence they leave.

ROSAURA: This is my sword, which unto thee alone
                    Must be surrendered, for of all those here
                    Thou art the noblest, and it may not be
                    Vouchsafed to one less gallant than thyself.

CLARÍN: Mine is such that it can be transferred
                    To one of lowest rank: here, take it, you! [*To a soldier*]

ROSAURA: And if I am to die, I want to leave
                    With thee, in gratitude for thy concern,
                    This token whose real worth derives from him
                    Who one day owned and wore it round his waist.

CLOTALDO: [*Aside*] Each instant my misfortunes grow apace.

ROSAURA: For this reason I beg thee keep this sword,
                    Because if fickle fate admits appeal
                    Of this harsh sentence, it will be the cause.
                    Although I do not know what secret it
                    Contains, I know it contains some secret.
                    It well might be that I'm mistaken, and
                    That I esteem it just because it is
                    My father's legacy.

CLOTALDO: And who was he?

ROSAURA: I never knew him.

CLOTALDO: Why didst thou come here?

ROSAURA: I come to Poland seeking to avenge
                    A grievance.

CLOTALDO: [*As he takes the sword he becomes upset.*]
                    [*Aside*] Holy Heaven! What is this?
                    My pain, confusion, anguish and despair

Grow even greater now. Who gave thee this?

[*To Rosaura*]

ROSAURA: A woman.

CLOTALDO: And what is her name?

ROSAURA: That I
Should not reveal her name is vital.

CLOTALDO: How
Dost thou infer or know, now, that there is
A secret in this sword?

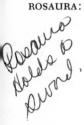

ROSAURA: The one who gave
It to me said: "Depart for Poland, and
Arrange through cleverness or artful stratagem
To have thy sword observed by nobles and
Important persons, for I know that one
Of them will favor and protect thee." But
In case he may be dead, she did not wish
To name him then.

CLOTALDO: [*Aside*]   May Heaven help me now!
What do I hear? I still cannot decide
If these events are just illusions or
Are really true. This is the sword I left
With lovely Violante as a pledge
That he who wore it round his waist should find
Me loving toward him as my son, and as
His father, kind. But what am I to do,
Alas, is such confusion, if the one
Who brings it as a token brings it for
His own undoing, since condemned to death
He stands here at my feet. What terrible
Confusion! And what miserable luck!

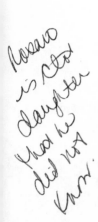

How fickle is one's fate! This is my son,
And his appearance harmonizes with
The summons in my heart, which, as it wants
To see him, flutters in my breast; and since
It cannot burst its bonds, it does just what
A person shut within a house would do
Who hears a noise out in the street, and peers
Out through the window; thus my heart, which does
Not know what's happening and hears a noise,
Peers out my eyes, which are the windows of
The soul, and makes its exit tearfully.
What shall I do? May Heaven help me! What
Am I to do? Because to take him to
The king is to take him (poor wretch) to die.
However, I cannot conceal him from
The king, by all the laws of fealty.
On one hand self-esteem, and loyalty
Upon the other: both hold me in thrall.
But why am I in doubt? The loyalty
I owe the king—does that not come before
Both life and honor? Well, may loyalty
Live on, and let him die. Besides, if I
Remember rightly what he said about
His coming to avenge a wrong, a man
Who bears a grudge is base. He's not my son,
He's not my son, nor has he my blue blood.
But if a danger has arisen now
From which no one is free—because honor
Is of such fragile stuff that just one touch
Will crack it, or a breath will tarnish it—

What else can he do, what else could one
Who is himself a noble do, except
To run these many risks and come to seek
It out? He is my son, he has my blood,
Since he has such great valor. So, between
These dual doubts, the mid-course that is most
Essential is to go before the king
And tell him that he is my son, and should
Be killed; perhaps the very sympathy
He has for my integrity may place
Him under obligation to me. And
If I deserve to have my son alive,
I'll help him to avenge his wrong; but if
The king persists in being harsh and kills
Him, he will die not knowing that I am
His father.
          [*To* ROSAURA *and* CLARÍN] Come you with
                              me, strangers, and
Do not have fears that you lack company
In your misfortunes, since in doubt like this
Concerning life or death, I do not know
Which one among us has the greatest woe. [*Exeunt*]

SCENE FIVE

*A hall in the Royal Palace at the capital. Astolfo and soldiers
enter from one side, and from the other Princess Estrella and
ladies of the Court. Military music and cannon salutes offstage.*

ASTOLFO: Most aptly, as they see those lovely eyes
            That sparkle like the rays of comets, both

complements

Drums and trumpets, birds and fountains, too,
Combine salutes that differ, but which have
A similar refrain, for with extreme
Amazement at thy heavenly aspect, some
Are turned to feathered trumpets, others are
As birds of brass; and thus they welcome thee,
Fair lady: guns salute thee as their Queen,
The birds as their Aurora,[4] trumpets as
Minerva,[5] and the flowers greet thee as
Their Flora,[6] for thou dost make mock of day
And banish night, Aurora in thy joy,
Flora in peace, Minerva in the fray,
And Queen that rules this heart of mine for aye.

ESTRELLA: If what one says is to be gauged by what
One's actions are, then thou hast done quite ill
In uttering such courtly flatteries
In which the lie is given thee by all
That panoply of war against which I
Take up bold arms; because, in my belief,
The honeyed words I hear from thee do not
Accord with the harsh actions that I see.
Observe, too, that it is a lowly deed
Fit only for a wild beast, and a source
Of fraud and treason, to be eloquent
In oral praise, and yet on murder bent.

skeptical of praise

contradiction

---

[4] Aurora: *Roman goddess of the dawn.*
[5] Minerva: *Roman goddess of wisdom, and protectress of prudent, courageous men in war.*
[6] Flora: *Roman goddess of gardens and the springtime.*

ASTOLFO:

Very badly hast thou been informed,
Estrella, since the faith of my fine words
Thou doubtest; and I beg thee hear me out
To see if I can state the case aright.
Upon the death of King Eustorgius
The Third of Poland, there remained as heirs
Basilio and two daughters to whom we
Were born. (I do not wish to bore thee with
Details that are irrelevant just now.)
Milady Clorilene, thy mother, who
Now in a better kingdom wears a veil
Of stars, was older, and you were her child;
The second daughter was my mother and
Your aunt, the lovely Recisunda (may
God rest her soul a thousand years); she wed
In Muscovy, and I was born to her.
To get back now to the beginning of
The tale is fitting. King Basilio,
Dear lady, is at present yielding to
The scorn that time shows for us all; inclined
More to his studies than to love, he is
A widower without a child, and we
Aspire to his throne. Thou dost allege
That thou art daughter to the elder of
The sisters; I, that I was born a male,
And though the younger sister's son, I ought
To be preferred to thee. Thy plan and mine
We told our uncle; he replied it was
His wish to reconcile us, and we set
This place and date. With this intention I

Departed from the land of Muscovy,
And with this same intention travelled here
Instead of making war on thee, so that
Thou couldst declare a war of love on me.
May Cupid, wise divinity, desire
The people (always right about these things)
To be prophetic in our case today,
Attaining this agreement in which thou
Wilt be the Queen, but also queen of my
Heart's choice; and as an added honor, our
Dear uncle will invest thee with his crown,
Thy valor shower triumphs upon thee,
And thou wilt conquer love's domain from me!

ESTRELLA: To gallantry so gracious my heart shows
Itself no less gallant, for just to make
Thee monarch of the Empire I could wish
That it were mine; although my heart is not
Convinced that thou art not ungrateful, for
Thy many words, I fear, are made false by
That picture pendant there upon thy breast.

ASTOLFO: To satisfy thee about it is my
Intention . . . But no opportunity
Is given by those many instruments

                                    [Drums offstage]
That sound, proclaiming that the king is now
About to come out with his parliament.

SCENE SIX

King BASILIO, *with his entourage.* ASTOLFO, ESTRELLA,
ladies-in-waiting, soldiers.

ESTRELLA: Wise Thales . . .[7]

ASTOLFO: Learnèd Euclid . . .[8]

ESTRELLA: Who among the signs . . .

ASTOLFO: Who among the stars . . .

ESTRELLA: Today dost rule . . .

ASTOLFO: Today dost live . . .

ESTRELLA: And their paths . . .

ASTOLFO: Their courses . . .

ESTRELLA: Thou dost describe . . .

ASTOLFO: Thou dost observe and measure . . .

ESTRELLA: Allow me in humble bonds . . .

ASTOLFO: Allow me in tender embrace . . .

ESTRELLA: To be like ivy clinging to thy trunk.

ASTOLFO: To be seen lying prostrate at thy feet.

BASILIO: Dear niece and nephew, come here to my arms,
And rest assured, since in compliance with
My fond command you come with such great love,
That I shall leave no one aggrieved, and that
You both are equal. So, when I confess
That I am bowed beneath the weight of years,
I call for only silence upon this
Occasion, since amazement will be called
For by the tale itself. You are aware
Already (be attentive to me, my
Belovèd niece and nephew, brilliant court

---

[7] Thales: *one of the Seven Sages of Greece, an astronomer and mathematician, born B.C. 640. Note these interlocking conversations, which must be read through individually to be intelligible. This was a favorite stylistic device of* culteranismo.

[8] Euclid: *celebrated mathematician who lived in Alexandria in the time of the first Ptolemy, B.C. 332-283. The speakers are flattering Basilio for his astronomical and mathematical abilities.*

Of Poland, vassals, kin, and friends) you are
Aware already that for wisdom I
Have earned abroad the surname "Learnèd," for
To outwit time and failing memory
The brush of Timanthes[9] and marbles of
Lysippus[10] in the compass of the globe
Acclaim me as Basilio the Great.
You know already that sciences are
My chief concern and what I most esteem:
Keen mathematics, through which I can take
From Time and break from Rumor their control
And function of revealing more each day;
For when upon my tablets I behold
As present the events of centuries
To come, I win men's thanks ahead of Time,
When later it reveals what I have said.
Those snow-white orbits, and those canopies
Of glass, illumined by the sun's bright rays
And pierced by the rotations of the moon;
Those spheres of diamonds and those globes
Of crystal that the stars adorn and that
The zodiac signs emblazon, form the great
Inquiry of my later years, and are
The books in which on diamond paper, in
Sapphire bindings, Heaven writes with lines
Of gold in divers signs our destinies,

[9] Timanthes: *celebrated Greek artist, who flourished about B.C. 400.*
[10] Lysippus: *distinguished Greek sculptor, contemporary of Alexander the Great, B.C. 356-323. These names are generic for artists and sculptors, as used here by Basilio.*

Adverse or kind. I read these with such speed
That with my spirit I pursue their swift
Excursions as they course the skyways. Would
To Heaven rather that my skill had been
A commentary in their margins and
An index to their pages; that my life
Had been the first debris demolished by
Their wrath, and that my tragedy had been
Contained within their bounds, because men marked
For melancholy suffer even through
Their very merits, since one who is harmed
By wisdom does indeed destroy himself.
Let me serve as an example, though
What has befallen me may be still more
Convincing; but to ponder these events
Again I ask of you a quiet ear.
By Cloriline, my wife, I had a son
Ill-starred: when he was born the heav'ns outdid
Themselves in wondrous signs. Before he left
The light to enter in the living tomb
That is a womb (because one's birth
And death are much alike), his mother, time
And time again, between reality
And raving, dreamed that she was giving birth
To some monstrosity in human form,
Who, stained in her own blood, was killing her
By being born, the human viper of
The century. The day arrived when he
Was to be born, and in fullfillment of
The omens (impious men are seldom or

Are never wrong) he came into this world *date*
With such a horoscope the sun turned red *of*
As blood, and furiously began to duel   *Birth*
The moon; and with the earth as their
Arena the two lamps of heaven fought
With thrusts of light, if not locked hand to hand.
The greatest and most horrible eclipse
The sun has ever suffered since it wept
Blood for the death of Christ was this
One, for the sun was drowned in living fire
And thought its last convulsion had arrived.
The skies grew dark, the buildings shook, the clouds
Rained stones, the rivers ran with blood. Then, in
This frenzy or delirium of the sun,
Prince Segismundo came into the world;
He gave some hint of his true nature then,
By causing his own mother's death, and said
With cruelty: "I am a man, since I
Already have begun to repay good
With evil." As for me, I hastened to
My books and in them, and in every sign,
I saw that Segismundo would turn out
To be a man most bold, a prince most cruel,
A monarch most ungodly, due to whom
The kingdom would divide against itself
And be a school for treason, an academy
Of vice. And he, swept on by his own
Great fury and by terrifying crimes,
Would trample over me, and I would find
Myself subdued beneath his feet (with what

A sense of shame I say it!) and the white
Beard of my face would be a rug for him
To tread upon. Who does not heed the threat
Of harm, especially the harm one has
Discovered in his study, where self-love
Prevails? So I, believing in the fates
That foretold harm in dreadful prophecies,
Determined to lock up the beast that had
Been born, to see if wisdom could outwit
The stars. It was announced the prince had died
At birth, and since I was forewarned, I had
A tower built among the rocks and crags
Of yonder mountains where the light has scarce
Found entrance, guarded by rough, jagged stones.
The heavy penalties and laws through which
The public was forbidden to set foot
In a restricted section of the hills
Were motivated by the reasons I
Have told you. Segismundo lives there in
A wretched, poor, imprisoned state, where just
Clotaldo has had contact with him; he
Has taught him science and the Christian faith,
And he alone has been a witness to
His sufferings. There are three factors here:
The first, that I, the King of Poland, love
You so, that I desire to free you from
Oppression and from being bound to serve
A tyrant king, because a sovereign who
Would place his fatherland and empire in
Such danger would be heartless. Secondly,

We must consider that if I deny
To my own son the right that every law,
Both human and divine, has given him,
This is not Christian charity; because
There is no law that says in order to
Restrain another from becoming harsh
And autocratic that I may be so
Myself; that if my son's a tyrant, to
Prevent him from committing crimes then I
Should perpetrate these very crimes myself.
The third and final factor is to see
How great an error it has been to give
Too much belief to the events foretold:
For though his disposition may dictate
His failings, these perhaps will not prevail;
Because the most determined destiny,
The most insistent inclination, and
The most pernicious planet can but bend
The will, not force it. So, irresolute
And hesitant to say what is the cause,
I have prescribed a remedy of such
A nature that it will astound you all.
Tomorrow, without telling him he is
My son—and your king—Segismundo (for
That is what we named him), I shall place
Him on my dais and my throne; in short,
He will replace me, govern and command
You there, and you will bow and swear to be
Obedient; thus I shall achieve three things,
With which I answer those three others that

Basilio Has 3 reasons.

Basilio will not will Segismundo out

a test Before
granting the throne
to By
astolfo &
estrella

I mentioned. First, if he is wise, discreet
And kind, refuting all the horoscope
Has said about him, you shall hail
Your rightful Prince, whose court has been among
The hills, his neighbors the wild animals.
The second is, if he is haughty, bold,
Defiant, cruel, and gives free reign to all
His vices, I shall then have piously
Fulfilled my obligation, and when I
Remove him I shall be behaving like
A king most resolute, for to return
Him to his cell will not be cruelty
But punishment. The third is, if the prince
Is as I have described, then through the love
I bear you all, my vassals, I shall give
To you a king and queen more worthy of
The crown and sceptre, for my nephew
And my niece, combining both their claims in one,
And pledged to holy wedlock, shall have what
They have deserved. I order this as king,
I ask it as your father, I entreat
You as a sage, and as your elder I
Proclaim it to you. And if Seneca[11]
The Spanish sage declared a king to be
The humble slave of his republic, then
As a slave I do beseech you this.

ASTOLFO: If it behooves me to reply, since I
Of all those here have been in fact the most
Concerned, I speak for everyone and say

---

[11] Seneca: *Roman moralist and philosopher, born in Spain about 4 B.C.*

Astolfo
agree to
Basilio

That Segismundo should come forth, for it
Suffices that he is a son of thine.

ALL: Deliver unto us our Prince; we want
Him for our king at once.

BASILIO: My subjects, I
Am grateful, and appreciate that kind
Expression. Lead my two supporters to
Their rooms; tomorrow you shall see him here.

ALL: Long live our gracious King Basilio!
[*All leave, accompanying* ESTRELLA *and* ASTOLFO;
the king remains.]

SCENE SEVEN

CLOTALDO, ROSAURA, CLARÍN, BASILIO

CLOTALDO: May I address Your Majesty? [*To the king*]

BASILIO: Ah, good
Clotaldo! Thou art welcome here indeed!

CLOTALDO: I need be so, perforce, to come before
Thy feet, for at this time, good sire, my sad
And stubborn fate breaks with the privilege
Of law and custom's use.

BASILIO: What troubles thee?

CLOTALDO: Misfortune, sire, has come upon me when
I might consider it the greatest joy.

BASILIO: Continue.

CLOTALDO: This fair youth, intrepid or
Else unaware, went in the tower, sire,
And there beheld the Prince. He is . . .

BASILIO: Do not
Distress thyself, Clotaldo; if it had

Clotaldo tells Basilio
that someone found
Segismundo

Been at some other time, I must confess
I would be angry, but I have revealed
The secret now; it matters not, since I
Have told it. Come to see me later, for
I have to tell thee many things, and there
Are many things that thou canst do for me.
Thou art to be—I give thee notice now—
The agent to perform the greatest deed
The world has seen. These captives (for I do
Not wish thee to suppose I penalize
Slight slips of thine) receive my amnesty.
[*He leaves*]

CLOTALDO: May thou, sire, live a thousand centuries!

SCENE EIGHT

CLOTALDO, ROSAURA, CLARÍN

CLOTALDO: [*Aside*] Heaven has improved my luck; now I
Shall not reveal he is my son: I can
Dispense with that.
[*To Rosaura and Clarín*] You foreign travellers
Are free.

ROSAURA: I hurl myself, beholden, at thy feet.

CLARÍN: And I, too, curl myself (one letter more
Or less means nothing between two good friends).

ROSAURA: Sir, thou hast given me my life, and since
I live because of thee, forever I
Shall be thy slave.

CLOTALDO: It is not life that I
Have given thee: a man of honor does
Not live with unavenged affronts; and since

Thou didst come seeking to avenge a wrong,
As thou hast told me, I have not preserved
Thy life, for thou didst come without one, since
A life·devoid of honor is not life.
[*Aside*] With that thought I shall stir him to
                    the quick.

ROSAURA: I must confess that I have none, although
From thee I do receive it now; but once
Avenged, my honor shall be so unstained
That then my life, despising dangers, shall
Appear to be a worthy gift from thee.

CLOTALDO: Take up the burnished steel that thou hast brought;
I know it will suffice, when stained red by
The blood of thine opponent, to give thee
Revenge, because a sword of mine (I mean,
A sword I've held in my possession for
A while) will know how to avenge thy wrong.

ROSAURA: In thy name for a second time I gird
It on, and on it swear to seek revenge,
Although my foe were powerful indeed.

CLOTALDO: And is he?

ROSAURA: So much so, that I do not
Declare it to thee, not because I do
Not trust thy prudence in important things,
But so thy sympathy and favor, which
Surprise and please me, may not be withdrawn.

CLOTALDO: Thou wouldst instead ensure my aid still more
By telling it, since that would close the door
To giving help to thine opponent. [*Aside*] Oh,
If I but knew his name!

ROSAURA: So that thou may'st
Not think I hold thy confidence in low
Esteem, know that my foe is none other
Than Astolfo, Duke of Muscovy.

CLOTALDO: [*Aside*] My grief is ill contained because, now seen,
The case is graver than I had conceived.
Let us inquire into it still more.
[*To Rosaura*] If thou wert born a Muscovite,
                                    the man
Who is thy rightful ruler hardly could
Affront thee; go back to thy country, then,
And set aside this fevered frenzy that
Incites thee.

ROSAURA: Even though he is my prince,
I know he could dishonor me.

CLOTALDO: He could
Not, even though he were to set his hand
Upon thy face. [*Aside*] Oh, heavens![12]

ROSAURA: The affront
To me was even greater.

CLOTALDO: Tell me, then,
For thou canst not say more than I surmise.

ROSAURA: I shall, yet I do not know why I gaze
At thee with such respect, regard thee with
Such great affection, look upon thee with
Such great esteem, that I cannot make bold
Enough to tell thee that this outer garb
Is but a fraud, since it does not befit

---

[12] *At this point Clotaldo realizes Rosaura's sex, because the only way royalty
could administer an affront to a subject was by dishonoring a woman.*

My person; judge, then, if I am not what
I seem, and if Astolfo came to wed
Estrella, whether he is able to
Dishonor me. I have told thee too much.

[*Exeunt* ROSAURA *and* CLARÍN.]

CLOTALDO: Please listen! Wait! Please stay! What labyrinth
Is this, where raveled reason cannot find
The thread? It is my honor that is stained,
And fearsome is the foe. A vassal I,
And she a woman; may a way be found
Through Heaven's help, although I do not know
If that can be, when in this mad abyss
All Heaven warns that all the world's amiss.

ACT TWO

SCENE ONE

BASILIO, CLOTALDO

CLOTALDO: All orders have been carried out as thou
        Didst bid.

BASILIO: Clotaldo, tell me how things went.

CLOTALDO: In this way, sire; the tranquillizing draught
        That thou didst order to be made, full of
        Ingredients combining properties
        Of several herbs whose overwhelming pow'r
        And secret strength deprives a mortal of
        His reason and transforms a man into
        A living corpse, and whose great potency
        Holds him so sound asleep his faculties
        And powers are completely gone . . . (we have
        No need to question that this can occur,
        My lord, for many times experience
        Has proved it to us, for it is a fact
        That medicine is full of Nature's lore
        And that there is no plant or animal
        Or stone that hasn't its fixed properties;
        And if our human malice can succeed
        In finding countless poisons that can kill,
        What wonder, if their strength can be controlled,
        That there be drugs to produce sleep as well
        As death? But leaving to one side all doubt
        That it can happen, for it is confirmed

By precept and by practice . . .) And so, with
The draught prepared of opium, poppy and
The henbane plant, I went down to the cell
Of Segismundo; there, I spoke with him
A while of human knowledge taught him by
Mute Nature through her hills and heavens,
And in whose hallowed halls he learned the speech
Of birds and beasts. In order to uplift
His spirit more to undertake the plan
Thou dost propose, I took the topic of
A mighty eagle which, despising the
High region of the winds, was climbing to
The highest strata like a feathered flash
Of lightning, or a shooting star. I praised
Its lofty flight and said, "Thou art, in fine,
The monarch of the birds, and it is right
That thou art so." He had no need of more,
For on this matter of his royalty
He talks at length with zeal and pride, because
In short, his blood incites him, stirs and moves
Him to great things. He said, "So even in
The restless realm of birds there is someone
To make them swear obedience! As I reach
This point, my own misfortunes give
Me consolation, for at least if I
Am prisoner, I'm forced to be, because
Of my free will I never would bow down
To any other man." Upon observing that
He had become infuriated now
With this theme, which has always been the source

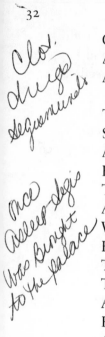

Of his great grief, I offered him the drink;
And scarcely had the potion left the glass
And been gulped down, his strength ebbed fast
                                    in sleep
Through all his limbs and veins a cold sweat spread,
So that if I had not known that it was
A counterfeit of death, I would have feared
His life was ended. At this point the men
To whom thou art entrusting this test came,
And in a carriage brought him to his room,
Where all the regal grandeur that befits
His person is in readiness. There in
Thy bed he has been placed, asleep, until
The time the lethargy has lost its hold,
And then they will attend him, sire, as if
He were thyself, for thus thou hast decreed.
And if my service merits some reward
From thee, the only thing I ask (if thou
Wilt pardon my presumption) is that I
Be told what purpose thou dost have
In bringing Segismundo to the palace thus?

BASILIO: Thy curiosity, Clotaldo, is
Quite proper, and to thee alone I would
Give satisfaction. Segismundo (this
Thou knowest fully) as my son lives in
Dire danger of untold misfortunes and
Disasters on account of his ill-starred
Predestination; and I want to see
If Heaven—and it cannot possibly
Be wrong, since we have had so many signs

Of violence in his cruel temper—
Has softened or become at least less harsh,
And, swayed by courage and discretion, has
Relented: men are masters of their fate.
I wish to test this, bringing him to where
He will find out he is my son, and where
He will give proof of his true character.
If he shows self-control and passes this,
He will be king; but if he proves himself
To be a cruel tyrant, I shall put
Him back into his chains. Now thou wilt ask,
For this experiment why did we need
To bring him fast asleep this way? And I
Shall satisfy thee, giving answer to
Thine every question. If he were to learn
Today he is my son, and find himself
Tomorrow for a second time reduced
To prison and to wretchedness he would,
Because of his condition, lose his mind;
For, once he finds out who he is, what can
Console him? Thus I have desired to leave
The door, in case of failure, open to
Declaring all he saw was just a dream.
This way two questions are resolved at once:
The first is his condition, for when he
Awakes he will reveal himself in all
His thoughts and fancies; and the second is
The matter of his consolation, for
Although he now may find himself obeyed
And later be returned to jail, he can

[handwritten margin notes: "Test for Segis." and "He is a prince but not recognized as so"]

Believe he dreamed it all; and he will be
Correct in this, Clotaldo, for on earth
Everyone who lives, lives in a dream.

CLOTALDO: I shall not lack good grounds to demonstrate
That thou wilt not succeed, but there is now
No remedy: all signs would indicate
He is awake, and is approaching us.

BASILIO: I would withdraw; do thou, his tutor, go
Up to him and relieve his troubled state
Of mind by telling him what has occurred.

CLOTALDO: Then thou dost grant me leave to tell him this?

BASILIO: I do; perhaps if he learns what is really true,
The danger will be easier to subdue.   [Exit]

SCENE TWO

CLARÍN, CLOTALDO

CLARÍN: [Aside] To get in here it cost me four whacks from
A haughty guard all rigged out in his red
Regalia with a beard to match, but I
Just have to see the whole performance and
There is no view that's better than a man
Brings with him, without begging tickets from
A vendor; for at all these shows a poor
But clever rogue can bluff his way inside.

CLOTALDO: [Aside] This is Clarín, who serves that girl who is
Alas! a merchant of misfortune and
Who has imported here to Poland an
Affront to me. [To CLARÍN] Clarín, what is the news?

CLARÍN: It is, good sir, that thy great sympathy,
All ready to avenge Rosaura's wrongs,

Advises her to dress in proper clothes.

CLOTALDO: And that is wise, in order to avoid
               The least appearance of indecency.

CLARÍN: Some more news is that through a change of name,
               And wisely choosing that of thine own niece,
               She has today achieved such status that
               She now resides within the palace as
               A lady in Estrella's retinue.

CLOTALDO: It's quite right that I should, once and for all,
               Assume responsibility for her
               Good name.

CLARÍN: Still further news: she hopes, good sir,
               The opening and time will come for thee
               To vindicate her honor very soon.

CLOTALDO: That is a safe procedure, for it will
               Be time alone that sets the stage for these
               Affairs.

CLARÍN: More news: she is regaled and served
               Just like a queen because she is thy niece;
               And even though I came with her I am
               Half dead with hunger, and nobody cares
               About me, or considers that my name
               Clarín means "Trumpet," and if this Clarín
               Sounds off he can tell all that's going on
               Straight to the king, Astolfo and the fair
               Estrella. Trumpets and men servants are
               Two things that find it difficult to keep
               From blaring out, and it might be that if
               My silence should be broken this refrain
               Would blow: "A trumpet heard at break of day

Could not sound lovelier in any way."

CLOTALDO: Thy protest is legitimate, and I
Shall see that thy complaint is satisfied;
Until then, thou art in my service.

CLARÍN: Well,
Sir, here is Segismundo coming now.

SCENE THREE

Music and singing. Servants, handing clothing to SEGISMUNDO,
who enters as if stunned. CLOTALDO, CLARÍN.

SEGISMUNDO: Good Heaven help me! What do I behold!
Good Heaven help me! What do I observe!
I'm startled by it, but have little fear;
Believe it's true, but yet have many doubts.
Am I in such a gorgeous palace, and
Am I dressed in fine fabrics and brocades?
Am I surrounded by men servants who
Are so resplendent and attentive? And
Have I awakened from my sleep in such
A splendid bed? Am I among all these
Attendants who are helping me to dress?
To say that I am dreaming is a lie:
I know full well that I am wide awake.
Am I not Segismundo? Heaven, free
Me from this error! Tell me what it is
That happened to my fancy while I slept
That I now find myself here. But at all
Events, why should I raise these questions? Let
Them wait on me, and then let come what may.

[handwritten margin note: Awakened to a new existence]

1ST SERV'NT: *[Aside to* 2ND SERVANT *and* CLARÍN]
How sad he is!

2ND SERV'NT: Who wouldn't be if this
Should happen to him?

CLARÍN: I would not be sad!

2ND SERV'NT: Go up and speak to him now.

1ST SERV'NT: Shall they sing
Again? *[To* SEGISMUNDO]

SEGISMUNDO: No more; I don't want them to sing.

1ST SERV'NT: Since thou art so disturbed, I wanted to
Amuse thee.

SEGISMUNDO: I don't feel the need to ease
My grief through song; the only thing I liked
Was listening to the military band.

CLOTALDO: Your Highness, noble master, let me kiss
Your hand; I wish to be the first to pledge
Obedience.

SEGISMUNDO: *[Aside]* This is Clotaldo, but
How is it that the one who treated me
So badly while in prison now treats me
With such respect? What's happening to me?

CLOTALDO: With all the great confusion caused thee by
Thy new-found status, thou must surely have
A thousand doubts that trouble thy discourse
And reason; but I would deliver thee
At once from all of them insofar as
That may be possible. Thou shouldst know, sire,
Thou art a prince and heir apparent to
The throne of Poland; thou hast been withdrawn
And hidden to obey the harsh decree

Clot tells Segie the truth

Of Fate, which forecasts for this Empire, if
The royal laurel crowns thy noble brow,
A thousand tragedies. But trusting in
Thy prudence to prevail over the stars
(Because a man of iron will can dominate
His destiny), thou hast been brought here to
The palace from the tower where thou wert
Confined, while thou wert fast asleep. The king,
Thy father and my sovereign lord, will come
To see thee, Segismundo, and from him
Thou wilt find out the rest.

SEGISMUNDO: Why, thou base-born
And infamous, disloyal man! What more
Have I to find out after learning who
I am, in order to display from this
Day forth my pride and power? How hast thou
Betrayed thy country, hiding thus my rank
From me, against all reason and the law?

CLOTALDO: Oh, woe is me! Unhappy man !

SEGISMUNDO: Thou wert
A traitor to the law, a truckling toad
Unto the king, and most unkind to me;
For this the king, the law, and I, beset
By terrible misfortunes, do condemn
Thee to thy death at my bare hands!

CLOTALDO: But sire . . .

SEGISMUNDO: Let none of you attempt to stop me, for
It would be useless, and (by Heaven!) if
You step before me I shall throw you out
The window!

2ND SERV'NT: Fly, Clotaldo!

CLOTALDO: Woe to thee!
Such haughtiness as thou art showing me,
Thou showest in a dream, unknowingly.

2ND SERV'NT: But note . . .

SEGISMUNDO: Get out of here!

2ND SERV'NT: That he obeyed
His king.

SEGISMUNDO: If it's a matter of a law
That is not just, he ought not to obey
The king; and I was his own prince.

2ND SERV'NT: He had no right to question if it was,
A good or bad law. *TO DO as you are told*

SEGISMUNDO: I suspect thou dost
Not care about thy life, since thou dost keep
On arguing.

CLARÍN: The prince is right, and thou
Art very wrong.

2ND SERV'NT: And who gave leave for thee
To speak?

CLARÍN: I took it.

SEGISMUNDO: Who art thou, pray tell?

CLARÍN: A meddler, and I am a master at
My trade, the biggest busybody known.

SEGISMUNDO: 'Tis thou alone in this whole world so new
Hast pleased thy prince.

CLARÍN: A prince of pleasers, true,
And a pleaser of Prince Segismundo, too!

SCENE FOUR

ASTOLFO, SEGISMUNDO, *Servants, Musicians*

ASTOLFO: This day is happy, Prince, a thousandfold,
       For thou dost rise as Poland's sun and fill
       Our whole horizon with a radiant joy
       And splendor since thou dost come, like the sun,
       From out the deep recesses of the hills.
       Come out, then, and though shining laurels crown
       Thy brow so late, may they be ever green.

SEGISMUNDO: May God be with thee.

ASTOLFO: I regret that we
       Did not become acquainted earlier;
       The loss is mine. I am Astolfo, born
       The Duke of Muscovy, thy cousin; we
       Should treat each other equally.

SEGISMUNDO: If I
       Say "God be with thee," do I not treat thee
       With courtesy enough? But since thou dost
       Prefer to boast of who thou art and make
       Complaint of this, the next time thou dost see
       Me I shall say "May God not be with thee!"

2ND SERV'NT: [*To* ASTOLFO]
       Consider, Highness, that he was born in
       The wilderness, and has behaved like this
       To everyone.
       [*To* SEGISMUNDO] Astolfo, sire, deserves . . .

SEGISMUNDO: It was annoying to me that he came
       To speak so formally, and the first
       Thing that he did was to put on his hat.

2ND SERV'NT: He is a grandee.[13]

SEGISMUNDO: I am grander still.

2ND SERV'NT: But even so, between you two it would
              Be better to show even more respect
              Than toward the others.

SEGISMUNDO: And who asked thy views?

SCENE FIVE

ESTRELLA *and the others enter*

ESTRELLA: Sire, may Your Highness be most welcome here
             Upon the throne that gratefully receives
             And wants you, and on which may you,
             August and famous, reign despite all false
             Predictions; may your life be counted here
             By centuries and not by years.

SEGISMUNDO: [*To* CLARÍN]   Now, tell
             compliment Me who this regal beauty is? Who is
             This human goddess at whose feet divine
             The very heavens lay their radiance? Who,
             Pray, is that lovely woman?

CLARÍN: Sire, it is
             Thy cousin who is named Estrella, which
             Means "Star."

SEGISMUNDO: Thou shouldst have called her "Sun."
             [*To* ESTRELLA] Though it is good to get good wishes
                                    for
             The good that's come to me, the only good
             That I admit is meeting thee today.
             And so, because I find myself with such

---

[13] *A grandee of Spain was the only person authorized to keep his hat on in the presence of royalty.*

Unmerited good fortune, thy good wish
Is thankfully received, Estrella. Thou
Canst dawn and bring joy to the brightest star.
If day breaks when thou dost arise, what dost
Thou leave the sun to do? Then let me kiss
That hand of thine, within whose snowy cup
The morning breeze doth sip its pale white glow.

ESTRELLA: Restrain thyself and be more courteous, please.

ASTOLFO: [*Aside*] If he should touch her hand, I'm lost!

2ND SERV'NT: [*Aside*] I know Astolfo's grief, and will stop this.
[*To* SEGISMUNDO] Please notice, sire, that it is not
                                    quite right
To be so bold, and with Astolfo here . . .

SEGISMUNDO: Have I not told thee not to interfere
With me?

2ND SERV'NT: What I am saying is but just.

SEGISMUNDO: All this makes me angry. Anything
Against my wishes seems unjust to me.

2ND SERV'NT: But I, my lord, have heard thee say thyself
That what is just should be obeyed and served.

SEGISMUNDO: Thou also heard'st me say that I shall hurl
Down from the balcony the man who dares
To vex me.

2ND SERV'NT: With a man like me that can't
Be done.

SEGISMUNDO: Oh, no? By Heaven, I shall have
A try at it!
[SEGISMUNDO *picks him up bodily and goes offstage;
all follow him, and return immediately.*]

ASTOLFO: What is this that I see?

ESTRELLA: Go stop him, all of you!   [*Exit*]

SEGISMUNDO: [*Returning*]   He hurtled from
            The balcony into the water. So,
            By Heaven, it was possible to do!

ASTOLFO: Thou really shouldst control thy violent
            Behavior, for between a man and beast
            There is a difference great as that between
            A palace and a mountain.

SEGISMUNDO: Maybe if
            Thou dost persist in lecturing like that,
            Thou mayst not have a head to hold thy hat!
                                        [*Exit* ASTOLFO]

Segis threatens astolfo

SCENE SIX

BASILIO, SEGISMUNDO, CLARÍN, *Servants*

BASILIO: What happened here?

SEGISMUNDO: It's nothing; only that
            I hurled down from this balcony a man
            Who was annoying me.

Killed a man

CLARÍN: [*To* SEGISMUNDO]   Be warned, he is
            The King.

BASILIO: So soon it costs a life to pay
            For thy arrival, and on the first day?

SEGISMUNDO: He told me it could not be done, and I
            Have won the bet.

BASILIO: It causes me great grief
            That when I come here, Prince, expecting to
            Discover that thou hast been warned about
            Thy horoscope, and find thee conquering

The stars, instead I see thee in so great
A rage as this, and find the first thing thou
Hast done in these new circumstances is
A frightful act of murder. With what love
Can I embrace thee if I know thine arms
Are schooled in dealing death in their fierce grasp?
Who ever saw the naked dagger blade
That gave a mortal thrust, and felt no fear?
Who ever saw the blood-stained place at which
Some other wretch was slain, and felt no grief?
The bravest man reacts instinctively.
So I, perceiving that thine arms are here
The instrument of death, and looking down
Upon the bloody spot, recoil from them.
Although I thought to gird thy neck in fond
Embrace, I shall withdraw without this sign,
For I am fearful of those arms of thine.

Basilio doesn't want a hug from a man who has killed a man

SEGISMUNDO: Well, I can get along without it, just
As I have done without it up to now.
A father who can treat me with such great
Severity, and whose harsh character
Can keep me from his side and bring me up
From childhood like an animal, and treats
Me like a monster, and who seeks my death—
What difference does it make if such a man
Denies my right to be embraced, when he
Denies my right to be a man as such?

Seg is doesn't care

BASILIO: Would but to Heaven and to God I had
Not given thee a life at all, for then
I would not hear thy voice or see thy bold
Effrontery.

SEGISMUNDO: If thou hadst not, I would
              Have no cause for complaint against thee; but
              Once given, then I do have cause, since thou
              Hast taken it away; for though to give
              Is a superlatively noble deed,
              It is most base to give and take away.
BASILIO: A fine way to show me thy gratitude
              For finding thyself changed now from a poor
              And wretched prisoner into a prince!
SEGISMUNDO: Well, why should I thank thee for that? Thou wert
              A tyrant over my free will, and now
              If thou art old and failing, and dost die,
              What dost thou leave to me but what is mine?
              Thou art my father and my king; then all
              This grandeur Nature's law gives me by right.
              And even though entitled to it thus,
              I'm free of any obligation toward
              Thee; rather can I call thee to account
              To me for all the time thou didst deprive
              Me of my freedom, life, and honor; so
              Be grateful to me that I do not make
              Demands on thee, for thou art in my debt.
BASILIO: Thou art a bold and brash barbarian.
              The prophecy of Heaven was correct;
              Thus to Heav'n itself I now appeal,
              Thou haughty, vain, and insolent young man.
              Although thou knowest thine identity
              And hast found out the truth, and now dost see
              Thyself preferred above all others in this place,
              Observe my warning carefully: be mild
              And gentle. This perhaps is thy mistake:

Thou may'st be only dreaming, not awake. [*Exit*]

SEGISMUNDO: I may be only dreaming, not awake?
I can't be dreaming, for I feel things; and
I know what I have been, and what I am.
And even though thou shouldst repent right now,
It would avail thee little; I know who
I am, and thou canst not (despite thy sighs
And sorrows) take from me the fact that I
Was born the heir apparent to this crown.
If thou didst hold me first in durance vile,
It was because I did not know my state;
But now I know just who I am—and find
That I am both a man and beast combined!

SCENE SEVEN

ROSAURA, *dressed as a woman*; SEGISMUNDO, CLARÍN, *Servants*

ROSAURA: [*Aside*] I come here following Estrella, and
I am in greatest fear that I may find
Astolfo, for Clotaldo does not want
Him to discover who I am, or see
Me; he insists it is important to
My honor. And I trust Clotaldo's good
Intentions: I am grateful to him for
Defending here my honor and my life.

CLARÍN: [*To* SEGISMUNDO]
What is it that has pleased thee most, of all
The things here thou hast seen and wondered at?

SEGISMUNDO: I've been amazed at nothing, for I had
Foreseen it all; but if I've wondered at

One thing I've seen here in this world, it is
The beauty of a woman. Once I read
In books I had that God devoted most
Attention to creating man, who is
A little world; but I suspect it was
To the creation of a woman, for
She is a little Heaven, and exceeds
Man's beauty by an astronomical
Amount. And more, if she is this one I
Am looking at.

ROSAURA: [*Aside*]   The prince is here; I'll leave.

SEGISMUNDO: Please listen, woman! Stop! Do not merge dusk
With dawn by leaving right away: for if
Thou wert to bring too close the light of morn
And sunset's chilly shadows, thou wouldst thus
Curtail my day. But what is this I see?

ROSAURA: I doubt, and yet believe my very eyes!

SEGISMUNDO: [*Aside*] I've seen this beauty somewhere.

ROSAURA: [*Aside*]   I have seen
This haughty grandeur held in durance vile.

SEGISMUNDO: [*Aside*] I've found my love at last.

[*To* ROSAURA]   Woman—because
That is the most endearing term a man
Can use—who art thou? Without knowing thee
I am in love, and so I claim thee just
On faith alone, for I am sure I've seen
Thee once before. Fair woman, who art thou?

ROSAURA: [*Aside*] I must pretend.
[*To* SEGISMUNDO]   I'm just a hapless maid,
A member of Estrella's retinue.

SEGISMUNDO:Say no such thing; say, rather, that thou art
The sun from which Estrella doth derive
Her star-like qualities, since she receives
Her splendor from thy rays. I have observed
That in the fragrant flower realm the rose
Doth reign as empress, goddess-like, because
She is the loveliest; I have observed,
Among the precious stones, the diamond
Presides in their learnèd academy
Of mines, and reigns as their own emperor
Because he is the most brilliant; I have
Observed, in those resplendent clusters of
The restless realm of stellar space, in first
Place, as their king, the morning star; I have
Observed the planets, called together by
The sun, in perfect spheres, and he held sway
O'er all, the greatest oracle of day.
How is it then that if among all these—
The flowers, stars and stones, the firmament
And planets—the most beautiful prevail,
Thou art in service to the one who has
Less beauty, and art lovelier than those:
The sun and stars, the diamond and the rose?

SCENE EIGHT

CLOTALDO, *who remains aside, listening;* SEGISMUNDO, ROSAURA,
CLARÍN, *Servants*

CLOTALDO: [*Aside*] To quiet Segismundo falls to me:
In short, I reared him. But what do I see!

ROSAURA: I prize thy favor, but let my reply
Come from my spokesman, silence; for when wit
Is slow, he speaks best who best holds his tongue.

SEGISMUNDO: Thou may'st not leave: remain! How canst thou
wish
To leave me all in darkness in this way?

ROSAURA: I beg permission, Highness, to withdraw.

SEGISMUNDO: To go away with such abruptness is
To take permission, not to ask for it.

ROSAURA: But if thou dost not grant it, I expect
To take it anyway.

SEGISMUNDO: Thou wilt provoke
Me to become discourteous and crude,
Because resistance to my will is like
A cruel poison to my patience.

ROSAURA: But
Although that poison, full of fury, hate
And rage, may overcome thy patience, it
Could not—nor would it dare to—overcome
Respect, which is my due.

SEGISMUNDO: Now just to see
If fear can make thee lose thy beauty, for
I am much given to performing the
Impossible: today I hurled down off
That balcony a man who said that it
Could not be done; so likewise, just to see
If I can—such an easy thing to do—
I'll hurl thy virtue out that window too.

CLOTALDO: [*Aside*] These things are getting very much
involved.

What can I do, in Heaven's name, when now
Because of an insane desire I find
My honor is a second time at stake?

ROSAURA: Thy tyranny foreshadowed (truth to tell)
For this unhappy land such shocking deeds
Of crime and treason, wrath and death. But what
Else is to be expected of a man
Who is a human in name only, an
Unbridled, savage, cruel, haughty and
Barbaric butcher, born among base beasts?

SEGISMUNDO: So thou wouldst not thus reproach me, I
Was so polite to thee, believing that I might
Win thee thereby; but if I am what thou
Hast said, despite my speaking thus, then thou
Shalt have (by Heav'n!) full cause to call me so.
You, there! Leave us alone, and lock that door;
Let no one enter.

[*Exeunt* CLARÍN *and the* SERVANTS]

ROSAURA: [*Aside*]   I am lost!
[*To* SEGISMUNDO]   Take note . . .

SEGISMUNDO: I am a tyrant, and in vain dost thou
Attempt to move me.

CLOTALDO: [*Aside*]   Such unheard-of strife!
Yet I shall stop him, though it cost my life.
[*To* SEGISMUNDO] My lord, please heed me; look.
[*He advances*]

SEGISMUNDO: A second time thou hast provoked my wrath,
Decrepit, mad old man. Dost thou hold my
Harsh anger in such low esteem? How didst
Thou get here?

CLOTALDO: I was called here by
                  The sound of thine own voice to tell thee that
                  Thou shouldst control thyself a little more
                  If thou wouldst be the king, and that
                  Thou shouldst not be so cruel just because
                  Thou are the master here—so it would seem—
                  For after all this might be just a dream.

SEGISMUNDO: Thou dost provoke my rage when thou dost hint
                  At disillusionment. I shall now see
                  If this is dream or truth by killing thee.
                  [*As he starts to draw his dagger, Clotaldo restrains
                  him, and then kneels.*]

CLOTALDO: In this way I may save my life, I hope.

SEGISMUNDO: Remove thy daring hand from my steel blade!

CLOTALDO: Until help comes to stay thy hand and wrath,
                  I shall not let thee go.

ROSAURA: Good Heavens!

SEGISMUNDO: Let
                  Me go, I say, decrepit, crazy, crude
                  Assailant, or like this with my bare hands
                  I shall crush thee to death! [*They struggle.*]

ROSAURA: Help! Quick!
                  Come, all of you! Clotaldo's being killed!
                  [*Astolfo enters, and as Clotaldo throws himself at
                  his feet, steps between the two men.*]

SCENE NINE

ASTOLFO, SEGISMUNDO, CLOTALDO

ASTOLFO: But what is this, my noble prince? Is this
                  The way that such a valiant blade should stain

Itself, in blood already cold with age?

Restore thy sword all shining to its sheath.

SEGISMUNDO: When I behold it bathed in his base blood!

ASTOLFO: His life has taken refuge at my feet;

My having come must be of some help here.

SEGISMUNDO: Then let it help thee die, for in this way

I shall be able to avenge, with thy

Death, too, that past affront.

ASTOLFO: My own life is

At stake, hence I do not fight royalty.[14]

[*Astolfo draws his sword; they duel.*]

CLOTALDO: Don't strike him, sir!

SCENE TEN

Enter BASILIO, ESTRELLA, *and the royal retinue.*

SEGISMUNDO, ASTOLFO, CLOTALDO.

BASILIO: Well, why are swords drawn here?

ESTRELLA: [*Aside*] It is Astolfo! Woe is me! Oh, pain

Most grievous!

BASILIO: Now, then; what has happened here?

ASTOLFO: A trifle, sire, now that thou hast arrived.

[*They sheathe their swords*][15]

SEGISMUNDO: A lot, sire, even though thou hast arrived.

I have been trying to kill this old man.

BASILIO: Didst thou have no respect for those gray hairs?

---

[14] *Astolfo avails himself of* la ley natural *(self defense) as his justification for fighting with royalty, the only possible excuse.*

[15] *In accordance with* la ley de la presencia real, *drawn swords must be sheathed when the king enters. The code then held that both sides had regained their honor, and that particular affair must never be resumed.*

CLOTALDO: They are but mine, and do not matter, sire.
SEGISMUNDO: How futile to expect that I should have
            Respect for graying hairs! Why, even thine
                                    [*to the king*]

*three to
Basilio*

            Could one day find themselves beneath my feet:
            I am not yet avenged to make thee pay
            For rearing me in such an unjust way. [*Exit*]
BASILIO: Before that happens thou wilt sleep again
            Where all that has occurred to thee will seem,
            Like all this world's realities, a dream.
            [*Exeunt the king,* CLOTALDO, *and the royal retinue.*]

SCENE ELEVEN

ESTRELLA, ASTOLFO

ASTOLFO: How rarely does fate lie when it foretells
            Misfortune, for it is as right when it
            Predicts bad luck as wrong when it portends
            Good prospects! What an apt astrologer
            A man would be if he were always to
            Make pitiless predictions, for there is
            No doubt they would be always accurate!
            The proof of this experiment can be
            Observed in Segismundo and in me,
            Estrella, for it shows two different
            Results. For him the fates foresaw but dire
            Disturbances, disdain, dejection, death:
            And they foretold the truth in every way,
            For all of it, indeed, is taking place.
            For me, however, when I saw those eyes
            So flashing that the sun was but a shade,

My lady, and the heavens but a cloud,
Predictions were for pleasure, prizes, palms
And property; the fates were wrong, yet right,
Since it is only natural that they
Should prove to be correct when making plain
Their favor—and according their disdain!

ESTRELLA: I have no doubt those gallantries are true
Enough, but they must be for someone else
Whose picture in a pendant round thy neck,
Astolfo, thou wert wearing when we met.
Since that is so, those compliments belong
To her alone. Go quickly to her that
She may repay thee; at the Court of Love
Invalid as credentials are nice things
Like gallant words for other ladies and
The loyal service rendered other kings.

SCENE TWELVE

ROSAURA, *who stands to one side;* ESTRELLA, ASTOLFO

ROSAURA: [*Aside*] Thank Heaven that my cruel misfortunes have
At last reached an extreme, for one who sees
This, has no further fears!

ASTOLFO: [*To Estrella*]   That portrait I'll
Remove, and to replace it I shall put
A picture of thy beauty; where the bright
Estrella glows, dark shadows find no place,
Just as the sun obliterates the stars.
I'll go and get it.
[*Aside*]   Pardon this offense,

My fair Rosaura; when they are apart
All men and women are untrue like this. [*Exit*]
[*Rosaura steps forward*]

ROSAURA: [*Aside*] I could not hear a word they said, for I
Was fearful he might see me.

ESTRELLA: Astrea!

ROSAURA: My lady?

ESTRELLA: I'm delighted that thou art
The one who came here, for it is to thee
Alone I'd tell this secret.

ROSAURA: Thou dost do
Great honor, lady, to one who serves thee.

ESTRELLA: Astrea, in the short time I have known
Thee, thou hast won my fullest confidence;
Therefore, and for thine own fine qualities,
I dare confide in thee some things that I
Have often hidden even from myself.

ROSAURA: I am thy servant.

ESTRELLA: Well, to be quite brief:
Astolfo, my first cousin (and I say
First cousin, for some things are plainly said
Through thoughts alone), is soon to marry me,
That is, if fortune wishes to repay
My many sorrows with one happiness.
It grieved me that the first day when we met
He wore about his neck the picture of
Some lady; I quite gently chided him;
He is gallant and chivalrous, so he
Has gone to get it, and will bring it here.
I'm most embarrassed that he's coming soon

[handwritten marginal note: Estrella Take Rosaura into her confidence]

To give it to me. Stay thou here, and when
He comes request him to give it to thee.
I say no more; discreet and fair thou art,
And must know well these matters of the heart.

                                        [*Exit*]

SCENE THIRTEEN

ROSAURA: If only I did not know! Heaven help
Me! Who is there so calm and wise that she
Would know how to advise herself today
In such disastrous circumstances? Can
There be a person in this world who is
More harassed by an unkind fate, or is
Besieged by greater griefs? What shall I do
In such confusion, where it seems that I
Can find no possible way out, and no
Way out that brings me consolation? Since
The first misfortune, there has been no deed
Or accident that has not led into
The next misfortune, for they follow close
Upon each other in succession, and
Are born one from the other, phoenix-like,
The living nourished from the dead within
A tomb kept always warm with ashes. Once
A wise man called misfortunes cowards, for
It seemed to him that they would never come
Alone; but I say they are brave, for they
Continue to advance and never turn
Away. A person who has them with him

Can dare do everything, for in no case
Should he fear that they may abandon him!
And I can say it, for so many things
Have happened to me and I never have
Discovered that I lacked misfortunes, nor
Have they relented to this day, when I
Now find myself undone by fate and in
The grasp of death. Oh, woe is me! What should
I do right now in this predicament?
If I tell who I am, Clotaldo may
Be angry with me—and I owe him my
Support and loyalty: he saved my life.
He bids me wait the satisfaction of
My honor silently. If I do not
Inform Astolfo and he finally
Does see me, how can I pretend? Because,
Although my voice and tongue and eyes may try,
My very soul will tell him that they lie.
What shall I do? But then, why do I plan
My actions? It is evident, despite
Precaution, study, and much thought, that I
Shall do what grief dictates when finally
The time arrives, for no one can control
His sorrows. Since the spirit does not dare
Determine what to do, let grief today
Reach new extremes, let sorrow reach new depths,
But let me cease, at last, to be afraid;
Until then, Heaven, I beseech thine aid.

SCENE FOURTEEN

ASTOLFO, *bringing the picture;* ROSAURA

ASTOLFO: This, my lady, is the picture; but . . .
Good God!

ROSAURA: Why does Your Highness stop? Why so
Surprised?

ASTOLFO: To hear and see thee, Rosaura.

ROSAURA: Rosaura? I? Your Highness errs if you
Confuse me with another lady, for
I am Astrea, and my humble state
Does not deserve such joy as causing you
To be upset because of me.

ASTOLFO: Enough,
Rosaura; you may try deception, but
One's soul can never lie, and though it sees
Thee as Astrea, as Rosaura it
Loves thee.

ROSAURA: I did not understand a word,
Your Highness, so I do not know just how
To answer; I can only say one thing:
Estrella (who can vie with Venus as
A star) told me to wait here for you, and
On her behalf to tell you that you should
Give her that picture—which is but a fair
Request—through me; and I myself shall take
It to her. This is what Estrella wants,
And even though it be her slightest whim
And to my disadvantage, it is she
Who wants it.

ASTOLFO: Make as many efforts as
Thou canst, Rosaura, but how badly thou
Dost feign! Please tell thine eyes to match their song
With thy sweet voice, for it is natural
That such an instrument be out of tune
In wishing to adjust the false notes that
Are spoken to the truth of what is felt.

ROSAURA: I only say that I am waiting for
That picture.

ASTOLFO: Inasmuch as thou dost want
To carry the deception to its end,
I'll answer thee in kind. Astrea, thou
Shalt tell the Princess I esteem her so,
That if she asks me for a picture it
Would be quite impolite to send her just
A copy; hence, in order that she may
Esteem and prize it, I am sending the
Original. And thou canst take it to
Her right away, since thou dost carry it
With thee, as thou dost carry thine own self.

ROSAURA: A man who is audacious, haughty, bold,
And eager to achieve his purpose, though
He be enticed by something that's worth more
If he returns without accomplishing
His end, feels foolish and frustrated. I
Have come to get a picture, and although
I bring back an original worth more,
I shall return frustrated; so give me
That picture now, Your Highness, for without
It I will not return.

ASTOLFO: But how, if I
Do not surrender it, art thou to take
It back?

ROSAURA: If that's the case . . . Let go of it,
You ingrate! [*She tries to take it from him.*]

ASTOLFO: It is hopeless.

ROSAURA: As God lives,
It shall not reach another woman's hands!

ASTOLFO: Thou art a fury!

ROSAURA: Thou art treacherous!

ASTOLFO: That is enough, Rosaura mine.

ROSAURA: I, thine?
Thou wretch, that is a lie!
         [*Both stand clutching the picture*]

SCENE FIFTEEN

ESTRELLA, ROSAURA, ASTOLFO

ESTRELLA: Astrea! And
Astolfo! What is this?

ASTOLFO: [*Aside*]   Estrella's here!

ROSAURA: [*Aside*] May love grant me the ingenuity
To get my picture back. [*To Estrella*] My lady, if
Thou dost desire to find out what this means,
I shall tell thee.

ASTOLFO: [*Aside to Rosaura*] What dost thou aim to do?

ROSAURA: Thou didst bid me await Astolfo here
And ask him for a picture for thee. I
Was all alone, and as one's thoughts flit here
And there so easily, and since I heard
Thee speak of pictures, it reminded me

That I had one of mine inside my sleeve.
I wanted to examine it, because
A person who's alone can be amused
By trifles; from my hand it dropped down to
The ground. Astolfo, coming to give thee
The picture of some other lady, picked
It up; and so reluctant is he to
Surrender what thou hast requested that
Instead of giving one, he wants to keep
The other, too; I cannot get mine back
By pleading or persuasion. Angry and
Impatient, I desired to snatch it back.
The one he has there in his hand, pray see,
Is mine: a glance will show it looks like me.

ESTRELLA: Astolfo, let the picture go.

> [*She takes it from his hand.*]

ASTOLFO: Madame . . .

ESTRELLA: The colors do not play thee false, in truth.

ROSAURA: Is it not mine?

ESTRELLA: Is there the slightest doubt?

ROSAURA: Now bid him give the other one to thee.

ESTRELLA: Here is thy picture; go.

ROSAURA: [*Aside*]   Well, anyway,
I've got my picture; now let come what may. [*Exit*]

SCENE SIXTEEN

ESTRELLA, ASTOLFO

ESTRELLA: Now let me have the picture that I asked
Of thee; for though I don't intend to see
Or speak to thee again, I do not want

It to remain in thy possession, if
For no more reason than I asked thee for
It foolishly.

ASTOLFO: [*Aside*]   How can I free myself
From this dilemma?
[*To Estrella*]   Even though I wish
To serve thee and obey thee, beautiful
Estrella, I shall be unable to
Give thee the picture thou dost seek, because . . .

ESTRELLA: Thou art a wretched and discourteous
Admirer. Now I do not want it from
Thee, for I never want thee to remind
Me, if I take it, that I asked for it.   [*Exit*]

ASTOLFO: Hear me! Listen! Look! Take note . . . !
Oh, Heav'n!
Rosaura, whence and how and why hast thou
Reached Poland for our mutual ruin now!   [*Exit*]

SCENE SEVENTEEN   *Backinthecave*

The Prince's prison in the tower. SEGISMUNDO, *as at the beginning, is wearing animal skins; he is in chains, and stretched out
on the floor.* CLOTALDO, *two servants,* CLARÍN.

CLOTALDO: Now leave him here, because today his pride
Will end where it began.

SERVANT: I'll fasten on
The chain again just as it was before.

CLARÍN: Do not awaken, Segismundo, to
Behold thine own undoing; luck has changed,
And all thy counterfeited glory was
A shadow of this life, a flash of death.

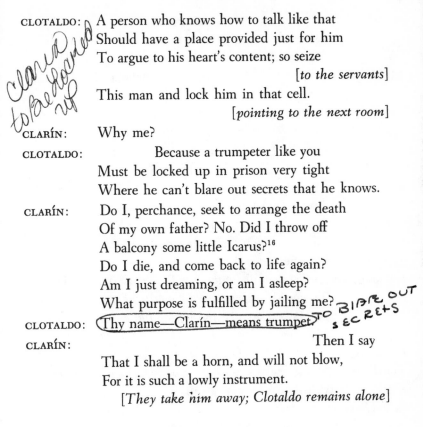

CLOTALDO: A person who knows how to talk like that
Should have a place provided just for him
To argue to his heart's content; so seize

[*to the servants*]

This man and lock him in that cell.

[*pointing to the next room*]

CLARÍN: Why me?

CLOTALDO: Because a trumpeter like you
Must be locked up in prison very tight
Where he can't blare out secrets that he knows.

CLARÍN: Do I, perchance, seek to arrange the death
Of my own father? No. Did I throw off
A balcony some little Icarus?[16]
Do I die, and come back to life again?
Am I just dreaming, or am I asleep?
What purpose is fulfilled by jailing me?

CLOTALDO: Thy name—Clarín—means trumpet.

CLARÍN: Then I say
That I shall be a horn, and will not blow,
For it is such a lowly instrument.

[*They take him away; Clotaldo remains alone*]

SCENE EIGHTEEN

BASILIO, *disguised*; CLOTALDO; SEGISMUNDO, *asleep*.

BASILIO: Clotaldo!

CLOTALDO: Sire! Your Majesty comes here
Like that?

---

[16] Icarus: *Daedalus' son, who flew too near the sun with wings fastened on with wax, and plunged to his death in the sea.*

BASILIO: My foolish curiosity
To see how Segismundo fares (alas!)
Has brought me here like this.

CLOTALDO: Behold him there,
Reduced to his abject condition.

BASILIO: Oh,
Unhappy Prince, whose birth was under stars
Ill-fated! Go and wake him up, now that
The draught he drank has robbed him of his
                                                  strength
And violence.

CLOTALDO: He's restless, sire, and talks.

BASILIO: Now what can he be dreaming of? Well, let
Us listen.

SEGISMUNDO:[*In his sleep*] Righteous is the prince who seeks
To punish tyrants. Let Clotaldo die
At my bare hands, and let my father kiss
My feet.

CLOTALDO: He threatens me with death.

BASILIO: And me
With violence and insult.

CLOTALDO: He intends
To take my life.

BASILIO: And plots to humble me.

SEGISMUNDO:[*In his sleep*]
Now let my peerless prowess enter on
The spacious stage of this great world playhouse;
So that my vengeance may be fitting, let
Them see Prince Segismundo triumph o'er
His father. [*He awakes.*] But, alas! Where am I now?

BASILIO: [*To Clotaldo*]
               He must not see me here; thou knowest what
               To do; I'll listen to him from back here.

                                          [*He withdraws.*]

SEGISMUNDO: Is it I, perchance, who find myself
               In captive chains in such a state? Art thou,
               O tower, not my tomb? Indeed thou art!
               Good Heav'n above! How many things I've dreamed!

CLOTALDO: [*Aside*] And now it is my turn to make believe.

SEGISMUNDO: Now is it time to waken?

CLOTALDO: Yes, it is.
               Art thou to spend the livelong day asleep?
               And hast thou not awakened since I left
               To follow that slow eagle in its flight
               Whilst thou remained behind?

SEGISMUNDO: I have not; and
               Not even now, Clotaldo, have I waked,
               For I believe that I am still asleep.
               And I am not far wrong, because if what
               Was dreamed, I saw and felt as real,
               Then what I see must be unreal; and it
               It not surprising that I dream awake,
               Since I can see when I am fast asleep.

CLOTALDO: Now tell me what it was that thou didst dream.

SEGISMUNDO: If I thought that it all was just a dream,
               I wouldn't tell it; but, Clotaldo, I
               Shall tell thee what I really saw. I woke
               To find myself (cruel illusion) in
               A bed that could—for shades and colors—be
               Compared with springtime's bed of blooms.

A thousand nobles, bowing at my feet,
Called me their prince and handed me rich robes
With jewels and decorations. Then thou didst
Completely change my calm to rapture when
Thou didst tell me of my good fortune: that
(Despite my present state) I was the Prince
Of Poland.

CLOTALDO: And I had, of course, a fine reward
For that.

SEGISMUNDO: Not fine at all, through treachery:
Both bold and strong, I tried to kill thee twice.

CLOTALDO: Such violence toward me?

SEGISMUNDO: I was the Lord
Of all, and took revenge on all. I loved
But one—a woman; that was true, I'm sure;
All else is gone, but that will e'er endure.
            [*The King withdraws.*]

CLOTALDO: [*Aside*] The King has left, much moved by what
                                he heard.

[*To Segismundo*] Since we were talking of that
                                eagle when

Thou didst drop off to sleep, thy dreams were of
High power; but in dreams it would be well
To honor him who brought thee up with care;
For, Segismundo, even sleeping tight
One should not lose one's sense of what is right.
                                     [*Exit*]

SEGISMUNDO:Quite so; then let us curb this temper and
          This fury, this ambition, lest perchance
          We are just dreaming; and indeed we will,
          For we are in a world so very strange
          That life is but a dream; experience
          Has taught me that each man who draws a breath
          Dreams what he is until he wakes in death.
          The king dreams he is king; believing this
          Illusion, he lives ordering, ruling,
          And governing; the borrowed plaudits he
          Receives are writ upon the wind, and Death
          (Sad fate!) converts them all to ashes. Who
          Is there would dare attempt to reign yet know
          He will awake in Death's cold dream laid low?
          The rich man dreams of riches, and they give
          Him greater cares; the poor man dreams that he
          Is suffering his wretched poverty;
          The man with new-made fortune dreams; the man
          Who is a social climber dreams; the man
          Who is offensive dreams; and in this world,
          In short, all men are dreaming what they are,
          Although nobody understands, by far.
          I dream that I am here, encumbered with
          These chains; I dreamed that I once found myself
          In yet another state more flattering.
          What is life? A frenzy. What is life?
          A shadow, an illusion, and a sham.
          The greatest good is small; all life, it seems,
          Is just a dream, and even dreams are dreams.

ACT THREE

SCENE ONE

In the tower. A cell next to SEGISMUNDO'S.

CLARÍN: In an enchanted tower, so it seems,
I live a prisoner. What will they do
To me because of what I do not know,
If they condemn me just because of what
I know? To think a man who always was
So hungry should, through living well, be put
To death! I'm sorry for myself! They all
Will say, "I told you so;" and well they may,
Because this silence doesn't quite befit
My name—Clarín—for I cannot refrain
From blaring out. My company in this
Place here, if I'm correct, consists of mice
And spiders. My, what sweet, dear birds!
Because of last night's dream my poor head rings
With oboes, trumpets, and parades of masques,
With crosses, and with flagellants; of these,
Some rise and others fall, some of them faint
On seeing blood upon the others. I,
However, faint from hunger, truth to tell.
For I discover that I'm in a jail
Where every day I read philosophy,
Half-starved, and every night I do not dine.
If they should some day name a new saint in
The calendar for keeping quiet, then

68

Saint Secret is my patron, for I fast
And do not feast upon his day; but then,
My punishment is well deserved, for I,
A servant, kept quite still—a sacrilege.
　　[Noise of drums, bugles, and voices offstage]

SCENE TWO

Soldiers, CLARÍN

1ST SOLDIER: *[Offstage]* This is the tower he is in! Knock down
　　　　　　The door, and everybody go inside!

CLARÍN:　　Good Heavens! They are certainly in search
　　　　　　Of me, because they say that I am here.
　　　　　　What can they want of me?

1ST SOLDIER: *[Offstage]*　　　　　　Go on inside!
　　　　　　　　　[Enter several soldiers]

2ND SOLDIER: Here he is!

CLARÍN:　　　　　　He isn't in.

SOLDIERS:　　　　　　　　　My lord . . .

CLARÍN:　　*[Aside]* These fellows are all drunk!

1ST SOLDIER:　　　　　　　　　Thou art our Prince;
　　　　　　We want and will accept none other than
　　　　　　Our native lord, and not a foreign prince.
　　　　　　Permit us all to kiss thy feet.

SOLDIERS:　　　　　　　　　Long live
　　　　　　Our own great Prince!

CLARÍN:　　*[Aside]* Good Heavens! They are serious! Is it
　　　　　　The custom in this kingdom to get hold
　　　　　　Of someone every day and make him prince,
　　　　　　And then return him to this tower? Yes,

Because I see it every day. Well, I
Must play my rôle.

SOLDIERS: Give us thy feet to kiss.

CLARÍN: I can't, because I need them for myself;
                  Besides, a footless prince would be no good.

SOLDIERS: We all have told thy father directly
                  That we will recognize no one but thee
                  As prince, and not the Duke of Moscovy.

CLARÍN: Have you all lost consideration for
                  My father? You are worthless fellows, all!

1ST SOLDIER: It was the loyalty that's in our hearts.

CLARÍN: If it was loyalty, I pardon you.

2ND SOLDIER: Come out, sire, and restore thy kingdom. Long
                  Live Segismundo!

ALL: We cheer him! Hurrah!

CLARÍN: [*Aside*] Do they say Segismundo? Well, that's good.
                  All fictitious princes have that name.

SCENE THREE

SEGISMUNDO, CLARÍN, *Soldiers*

SEGISMUNDO: Who is it here that calls my name?

CLARÍN: I am
                  Indeed a prince of hollow shams!

1ST SOLDIER: Then who
                  Is Segismundo?

SEGISMUNDO: I.

2ND SOLDIER: [*To Clarín*]   Then how didst thou,
                  So bold and foolish, dare to take his place?

CLARÍN: I, Segismundo? I deny that. You're

(margin note:) Poor Judgement

The ones that segismundized me, and so
The boldness and the foolishness were yours.

1ST SOLDIER: O great Prince Segismundo (for thou hast
The bearing of the titles we have brought,
Although on faith alone we do acclaim
Thee as our lord), thy father, mighty King
Basilio, is fearful lest the fates
Fulfill a prophecy that says he is
To find himself submissive at thy feet
And overthrown by thee, so he attempts
To take away thy claim and title due ,
By birth, in favor of Astolfo, Duke
Of Muscovy; to this end, he convened
His Court. The people, understanding now,
And knowing that they have a native King,
Do not want any foreigner to come
To rule them; and with lofty scorn of dire
Predictions, they have come to seek thee out
Where thou dost live a prisoner, so that
Thou may'st, assisted by their arms, escape
This tower and restore thy royal crown
And power, seizing them from tyrant hands.
Come out, then, sire, for in this desert waste
A mighty army of guerrillas and
Of commoners acclaims thee. Liberty
Awaits thee; listen to its accents free!

VOICES: [Offstage] Long live Segismundo! Victory!

SEGISMUNDO: Oh, Heaven, dost thou now desire that I
Should dream again of grandeur that will fade
With time? Dost thou desire me to glimpse

Again, amid the half-formed shadows, so
Much pomp and circumstance, gone with the wind?
Again dost thou desire me to feel
The disillusionment and shocks this flesh
Is heir to, and to which it lives alert?
It must not, no, it must not be, that I
Should find myself Fate's prisoner again.
And since I know that all this life's a dream,
Get hence, deluding shadows, feigning to
My deadened senses voice and substance, when
In truth you have no substance and no voice;
I want no make-believe magnificence,
Pretended pomp, or flights of fancy that
Will vanish at the merest breath of breeze,
Just like the almond tree in early bloom,
Whose flowers are all prematurely blown
Away, and then its buds, all blighted, lose
Their beautiful pink brilliant quality.
I know you all of old, I know your game;
To anyone who sleeps, you do the same.
For me, enchantment has no fatuous gleam:
I'm disabused, and know that life's a dream.

2ND SOLDIER: If thou dost think we are deceiving thee,
Just turn thine eyes toward those imposing hills
And see the people waiting thy command.

SEGISMUNDO: I have already seen that very thing
As clearly and distinctly as I see
It now, and it was just a dream.

He accepts his one day as a dream

2ND SOLDIER: Great deeds,
My noble lord, have always been foretold;
If thou didst dream it first, that was a sign.

SEGISMUNDO: Thou art correct, it was an omen; and
In case it's true, because this life is short,
Let's dream, my soul, let's dream again. But it
Will be with prior warning that perhaps
We shall awaken from this joy when least
Expected; thus our disillusionment
Will be less harsh, for we shall ease the pain
By this anticipation. Thus forewarned
That even though it seems assured, all of
Our power is just lent, and must return
Unto the Giver, let's risk everything!
My subjects, I am grateful to you for
Your loyalty. In me you follow one
Who boldly and with skill will free you all
From foreign slavery. To arms! You soon
Will see my dauntless valor. I intend
To take up arms against my father and
To prove the stars were right concerning me,
Since I shall see him prostrate at my feet . . .
[*Aside*] But if I should awake before that, might
It not be better not to mention it,
In case I am not fated to succeed?

ALL: Long live Segismundo! Victory!

Everything is Loaned by God

SCENE FOUR

CLOTALDO, SEGISMUNDO, CLARÍN, *Soldiers*

CLOTALDO: What tumult is all this, in Heaven's name?

SEGISMUNDO: Clotaldo.

CLOTALDO: Sire . . . [*Aside*] His wrath will fall on me.

CLARÍN: [*Aside*] I'll bet he throws him headlong off the cliff.
                                                    [*Exit*]

CLOTALDO: I come to thy royal feet, I know, to die.

SEGISMUNDO: Rise up, rise up, dear mentor, from the ground.
             Thou art to be the guiding light to whom
             I trust my efforts, for I know that I
             Owe my upbringing to thy loyalty.
             Embrace me now.

CLOTALDO: What dost thou say?

SEGISMUNDO: That I
             Am dreaming, and I want to do what's right:
             One should not lose that sense, though sleeping tight.[17]

CLOTALDO: If doing right is now thy object, sire,
             Thou surely wilt not be offended if
             I now suggest the same. Make war upon
             Thy father? I cannot be now thy guide,
             Nor serve against my king. I place myself,
             Submissive, at thy feet; now take my life.

SEGISMUNDO: Base villain! Traitor! Ingrate!
             [*Aside*]   It behooves
             Me, Heaven knows, to hold myself in check:
             I still don't know if I am wide awake.
             [*To Clotaldo*] Clotaldo, thou hast courage that
                                  calls forth
             My envy and my thanks. Go hence and serve
             The king; upon the field we'll meet again.
             [*To the soldiers*] Sound out the call to arms!

CLOTALDO: I kiss thy feet
             A thousand times. [*Exit*]

---

[17] *Segismundo quotes to Clotaldo the same words the latter used to him at the end of Scene 18 of Act II.*

SEGISMUNDO: On, Fate! We go to reign!
　　　　　Do not awaken me if I'm asleep;
　　　　　And if all this is real, please do not put
　　　　　Me back to sleep. But be it true or just
　　　　　A dream, to do right is what matters most.
　　　　　If this be true, then for those very ends;
　　　　　If not, that when we wake we may win friends.
　　　　　　　　　[*Exeunt, to the sound of drums*]

SCENE FIVE

BASILIO, ASTOLFO

BASILIO: Astolfo, who is there so strong that he
　　　　　Can check the fury of an untamed steed?
　　　　　And who can halt the mighty current of
　　　　　A river plunging headlong to the sea?
　　　　　Or boldly keep from falling down the cliff
　　　　　A boulder loosened from a mountain peak?
　　　　　Well, each of these is easier to stop
　　　　　Than the unbridled fury of a mob.
　　　　　Just spread a rumor in one faction, and
　　　　　It soon is heard to echo through the hills:
　　　　　"Astolfo!;" others "Segismundo!" cry.
　　　　　The throne-room, scene of such duplicity,
　　　　　Is now become the bloody stage on which
　　　　　Stern Fortune grimly acts out tragedies.

ASTOLFO: My lord, let all joy be postponed today;
　　　　　Let plaudits cease; defer the sweet delights
　　　　　Thy bounteous hand has promised me; for if
　　　　　This Poland, which I now aspire to rule,

Resists obeying me, it is because
I first must show my mettle. Let me have
A horse, and he whose scutcheon proudly shows
Such thunder will deliver lightning blows. [*Exit*]

BASILIO: There is no remedy for what has been
Decreed; moreover, there is risk in what
Has been foretold. If it is to occur,
Defense is hopeless; for the one who most
Would ward it off is he who most foresees.
Inexorable law! Heartrending case!
Appalling fate! That he who sought to shun
The risk should stumble on it! And to think
That I, by hiding him, have with this hand
Destroyed myself and my own Fatherland!

SCENE SIX

BASILIO, ESTRELLA

ESTRELLA: If thou in person, sire, dost not attempt
To check this tumult that has broken out,
With two opposing factions streaming through
The streets and public squares, thy kingdom will
Soon be engulfed and stained all scarlet in
A sea of blood, for now in some sad way,
Misfortune rules, and tragedy holds sway.
Such is the ruin of thy kingdom, such
The might of harsh and bloody violence,
That seeing it strikes awe and hearing it
Inspires fear. The sun is overcast,
The wind is stilled; each rock is now become
A gravestone, and each bloom is ready for

A floral wreath; each building now is but
A waiting sepulchre of mighty stones,
Each soldier but a corpse of living bones.

SCENE SEVEN

BASILIO, ESTRELLA, CLOTALDO

CLOTALDO: Thank Heaven that I reach thy feet alive!

BASILIO: How now, Clotaldo! Tell me, what's the news
Of Segismundo?

CLOTALDO: That the mob, all stirred
To blind and brutish passion, broke into
The tower, and out of its dungeon took
Their prince; as soon as he saw that he had
Again his former rank, he showed himself
To be relentless, and declared that he
Would boldly test the truth of prophecy.

BASILIO: Get me a horse, for I in person would
Stout-heartedly defeat this ingrate son.
And now as I defend my royal sway,
Where knowledge erred, may cold steel win the
day. [*Exit*]

ESTRELLA: I'll be Bellona[18] to our royal Sun,
And place my name beside his warlike one;
On outstretched wings this day I hope to soar,
And rival Pallas,[19] wise goddess of war.
[*Exit, as the call to arms is sounded*]

---

[18] Bellona: *Roman goddess of war.*

[19] Pallas: *Athena, Greek counterpart of the Roman Minerva, protectress of wise warriors.*

SCENE EIGHT

Enter ROSAURA, *who detains* CLOTALDO.

ROSAURA: Although the valor in thy breast cries out
To join the fray, give ear to me, for I
Know well that all of this is war. Thou art
Aware that I came here to Poland poor,
In lowly state, and most unhappy; then,
Protected by thy gallantry, I found
Compassion; thou didst order me to live
Disguised within the palace and to hide
My jealousy, attempting to avoid
Astolfo. Finally he saw and knew
Me, and—despite this—he so tramples on
My honor that tonight he is to meet
Estrella in a garden. I secured
The key to it, and so can furnish thee
The opportunity to go inside
And put an end to all my cares. And so
Thou canst with daring, boldness, and with strength
Restore my honor to me, since thou art
Determined to avenge me with his death.

CLOTALDO: It is quite true that when I met thee I
Determined then to do on thy behalf,
Rosaura, all within my power; thine
Own weeping was a witness. First I tried
To get that suit away from thee: in case
Astolfo saw thee he would see thee in
Thy proper dress, and would not deem unchaste
The rashness that caused thee to risk thy name.

And meanwhile I was planning how I could
Recover thy lost honor, even to
The point (thine honor meant so much to me)
Of murdering Astolfo. Such short-lived
Absurdity! However, he is not
My king, so this does not disturb me much.
I was about to kill him when just then
Wild Segismundo tried to murder me.
Astolfo, scorning danger, came to my
Defense, displaying sheer willpower and
Raw courage that surpassed all bravery.
Now how am I, with thankful heart,
To kill (note this) the man who saved my life?
And so with my affection and concern
Divided equally between you two,
Since I have given life to thee and have
Received my life from him, I do not know
Which party to befriend or to support.
Thou art obliged to me, and I to him,
For giving and receiving; therefore, in
This present action my love finds no cheer:
I am both plaintiff and defendant here.

ROSAURA: There is no need for me to tell thee that
What in a man of quality it is
A noble thing to give, is equally
Ignoble to receive. According to
This principle, thou ought not be obliged
To him, for if he is the one who gave
Thee life, and thou to me, it follows that
He forced thy noble nature to perform

A deed ignoble, while I caused thee to
Perform a noble deed. Therefore thou art
Aggrieved at him and duty-bound to me,
Since thou hast given me what thou didst get
From him. And therefore thou shouldst hasten to
The rescue of my honor in the same
Degree as I have merit over him
For causing thee to give, and not receive.

CLOTALDO: Although nobility derives from him who gives,
All gratitude stems from him who receives.
And since I've learned already how to give,
I'll have another claim to fame: I'll be
As generous as noble. Leave to me
The name of being grateful, for I can
Achieve it just as well by being so
As by my generosity, for it
Is just as great to give as to receive.

ROSAURA: From thee I did receive my life, and thou
Didst tell me at that time that life without
Respect is not a life; in that case, I
Received nothing from thee; no life at all
Is what thy hand has given me. If thou
Wouldst be more generous than grateful (as
I heard thee say), I hope thou wilt give me
The life thou hast not given yet; thou wilt
Be even greater, for if liberal
Before, thou wilt be later full of thanks.

CLOTALDO: Won over by thy reasoning, I shall
Be generous, Rosaura; I shall give
To thee my property; go thou to live

Within a convent. I present a plan
That has been well thought out: thou wilt
Prevent a crime, and find a refuge there.
For when the kingdom is beset and so
Divided, as a nobleman I shall
Not add to its unhappiness. With the
Solution outlined I am loyal to
The crown and generous to thee, as well
As grateful to Astolfo. Therefore choose
This remedy most fitting, which avoids
The two extremes. Lord knows I could not do,
If I were thine own father, any more.

ROSAURA: Wert thou my father, I would suffer such
Grave wrong, but since this is not so, I won't.

CLOTALDO: Well, what does thou intend to do?

ROSAURA: To kill
The Duke.

CLOTALDO: A lady who has never known
Her father has such bravery?

ROSAURA: I have.

CLOTALDO: What spurs thee on?

ROSAURA: My reputation.

CLOTALDO: Try
To see Astolfo as . . .

ROSAURA: A man who shames
My honor.

CLOTALDO: Thine own king, and husband of
Estrella.

ROSAURA: As God lives, he shall not be!

CLOTALDO: That's madness.

ROSAURA: Yes, I know it is.

CLOTALDO: Well, rise
Above it.

ROSAURA: I cannot.

CLOTALDO: Then thou wilt lose . . .

ROSAURA: I know.

CLOTALDO: Thy life and honor.

ROSAURA: Certainly.

CLOTALDO: What dost thou seek?

ROSAURA: My death.

CLOTALDO: But that
Is spite.

ROSAURA: It's honor!

CLOTALDO: Folly.

ROSAURA: Valor!

CLOTALDO: It
Is madness.

ROSAURA: It is rabid, raging wrath!

CLOTALDO: In short, there is no way to get control
Of thy blind passion?

ROSAURA: No!

CLOTALDO: Who is to help
Thee?

ROSAURA: I myself.

CLOTALDO: There is no remedy?

ROSAURA: There is no remedy.

CLOTALDO: Think well; there may
Be other ways.

ROSAURA: To cause my ruin, yes.   [*Exit*]

CLOTALDO: If thou art bent on ruin, daughter, wait;
Together let us boldly meet our fate.   [*Exit*]

SCENE NINE

The battlefield. SEGISMUNDO *is dressed in skins; soldiers are marching.* CLARÍN. *The sound of drums.*

SEGISMUNDO: If Rome amid the triumphs of its golden age
    Could see me now, how happy it would be
    On such a rare occasion when a fiend
    Would lead its mighty legions, and whose proud
    Self-confidence would deem the firmament
    Itself a minor conquest! But let us
    Not soar too high, my spirits, nor provoke
    These fickle plaudits to take flight;
    For if I am to grieve, when I awake,
    That I did gain them just to lose again,
    A smaller lot to lose would hurt less, then.
       [A bugle is blown]

CLARÍN: Astride a speedy mount (you will excuse[20]
    My coloring the scene as I relate
    The tale) on which a map is carefully
    Depicted, since his body is the earth,
    The heart within his breast is fire, his sweat
    The sea, his breathing is the air (at which
    Chaotic mixture I am all agog,
    Since in his heart and sweat, his body and
    His breath he is a monster made of fire
    And earth, of sea and wind)—astride this mount
    Of dapple gray, that seems to fly instead
    Of run, urged on by her who wields the spur,
    A lovely woman rides to meet thee, sir.

[20] *The comic's description of Rosaura's horse is in imitation of the affected style of the period.*

SEGISMUNDO: Her brilliance dazzles me.

CLARÍN: Good Lord! It is
Rosaura! [*He withdraws.*]

SEGISMUNDO: Heaven brings her back to me.

SCENE TEN

ROSAURA, *wearing a loose jacket, sword and dagger;* SEGISMUNDO;
soldiers.

ROSAURA: Kind Segismundo, whose heroic glow
                Comes forth from out the shadowed night into
                Its daylight deeds just like the sun, which in
                The arms of dawn returns all shining to
                The plants and flowers, and peers over hills
                And seas, all crowned with glory, spreading light
                And flooding rays upon the mountain peaks,
                And flecking all the foam with gold, may thou,
                O shining sun of Poland, dawn upon
                The world as thou dost now appear to this
                Unhappy woman who today prostrates
                Herself before thy feet in search of help,
                Because she is a woman and in need:
                These are two things that obligate a man
                Who prides himself on being chivalrous,
                For either of the two is quite enough,
                Nay, either of the two is more than that.
                Three times hast thou admired me, three times
                Hast thou not known just who I am, because
                On three occasions thou didst see me in
                A different dress and character. The first
                Time thou didst think I was a man; that was

When thou in durance vile did lead a life
That beggared my unhappiness. Then came
The second time, when thou didst stand aghast
To see me as a woman; that was when
Thy pomp and majesty were all a dream,
A fantasy, a sham. The third time is
Today, when I must seem a freak of both
The sexes in my feminine attire
And masculine accoutrements of war.
So that, if moved to pity, thou may'st be
More ready to defend me, it is well
That thou shouldst hear my tale of tragedy.
My mother was a noble lady of
The Court of Muscovy, who must have been
Extremely beautiful if we can judge
By her misfortune. Some betrayer saw
Her, and I do not speak his name because
I never knew him, but he must have been
Of rank, I feel within me; and, since I
Resulted from their union, I am moved
To madness at not having been born as
A pagan, so I might persuade myself
It was a god transformed into a rain
Of gold, a swan, or else a bull, that came
To Danae,[21] Leda,[22] or Europa[23] and
Did sire me. Although I thought that I
Was lengthening the story, citing tales

[21] Danaë: *mother of Perseus by Zeus, who came to her as a shower of gold.*
[22] Leda: *mother of Castor and Pollux by Zeus, who came to her as a swan.*
[23] Europa: *mother of Minos by Zeus, who took the form of a bull to carry her off.*

Of perfidy, I find that in it I
Have told thee briefly that my mother, more
Resplendent than all other women and,
Like all, unhappy, fell a victim to
Love's tenderest expression. That excuse,
So foolishly believed, about his faith
And promises of marriage touched her so,
That even to this day the thought of them
Upsets her to the point of tears; he fled
Just as Aeneas[24] did from Troy, and even left
His sword with her. His blade will stay here in
Its sheath until I draw it out before
The story ends. From this loose knot,
Which does not bind or hold, this marriage or
This crime (it all amounts to much the same),
I came into the world so much like her
That I was but her faithful image, not
In beauty, but in fortune and in deeds.
And so I have no need to say that I,
Unhappy heiress of her lot, have found
The same sad, stormy fate as she.
The most that I can tell thee of myself
Is that the one who stole the trophy of
My honor and the shreds of my good name
Is called Astolfo . . . Ah! When I but speak
His name my heart begins to boil with rage
The way it would when mentioning a foe.
Astolfo was the faithless lover who,

---

[24] Aeneas: *Calderón apparently overlooked the fact that Aeneas could not have left his sword with Dido when he fled Troy; it was at Carthage that he met her.*

Forgetting all his promises (because
When love is over even memories
Fade from the mind), came here to Poland for
His marriage to Estrella, evening star
That sparkled in the twilight of my love.
Who would believe that since it was a star
That smiled upon two lovers, it would be
Another star—Estrella—who would now
Divide them? I, offended and deceived,
Was left in sadness, left in madness, left
At point of death; left to myself, which is
To say that all the torments of the damned
Formed one great Babel of confusion in
My mind. Determined to be silent (for
One's deepest pains and sorrows are expressed
More truly by one's feelings than by words),
I inly wept; but then one day, alone,
My mother, Violante, burst the bonds
That held them pent within my breast, and they
All tumbled forth in one great rushing horde.
I felt no shame in telling of my trials,
For if a person knows the one to whom
She is confiding all her weaknesses
Has been involved in others of her own,
It seems to help her to unburden them.
At times a bad example has some use.
In short, she heard my woes with sympathy,
And tried to give me consolation with
Her own; how readily a judge who has
Committed indiscretions can condone!

Self-taught through sad experience, she saw
That leaving things to time or happenstance
Was not a remedy for honor's loss
In her own case, and felt the same was true
In my unhappiness. She thought the best
Advice would be to follow him, and by
Persuading him with gallantry, oblige
Him to fulfill his debt of honor; and,
So that it might be done at less risk to
Myself, fate would prefer that I should wear
The clothing of a man. She took down this
Old sword that I am wearing; now the time
I must unsheathe the blade is here at hand,
As I did promise. Trusting in its sign,
She said to me: "Depart for Poland and
Make sure this sword is seen upon thee by
The highest nobles, for in one of them
Thy cause will find a sympathetic ear,
Thy sufferings some consolation." Well,
I came to Poland; let us then omit
The fact (there is no need to mention it,
For it is known already) that a horse run wild
Brought me here to thy cave, where thou
Wert startled to behold me. Let's omit
The fact that here Clotaldo took my part
Most vehemently; that he asked the king
To spare my life, and this was granted him;
That when he found out who I was he asked
Me to put on my proper dress and go
To serve Estrella, where I cleverly

Upset Astolfo's plans for making her
His wife. Let us omit the fact that thou
Didst see me here again, this time dressed as
A woman, and that, all confused, thou didst
Mix up the two events. Let us get to
The fact that when Clotaldo was convinced
It was important to him that there be
A marriage of Astolfo with the fair
Estrella and the two should reign, against
My honor he advised me to discard
My claim. Since thou, brave Segismundo, hast
Today thy chance for vengeance (for it is
The wish of Heaven that thou shouldst escape
This rustic prison where thy body has
Been just a beast to human feeling and
A rock toward suffering), and dost take arms
Against thy father and thy land, I come
To help thee, mixing with Diana's[25] garb
The trappings of Minerva, wearing now
Rich cloth and steel, for both adorn
My person. On, then, bold commander! For
The two of us it is important to prevent
And then undo this marriage that they plan:
For me, so that the man who calls himself
My husband shall not marry; and for thee,
Because if their two states are joined they can,
With greater military force, cast doubt
Upon our triumph. As a woman, I
Have come here to persuade thee to redeem

---

[25] Diana: *Roman goddess of the chase.*

My honor; as a man I come to urge
Thee to redeem thy crown. As a woman
I come to soften thee as I prostrate
Myself before thy feet; and as a man
I come to serve thee with my sword and self.
But please remember: if thou dost attempt
To make love to me as a woman, as
A man I'll kill thee staunchly in defense
Of my good name; because I aim to be,
If someone tries to conquer my love's will,
A woman who will cry, a man who'll kill.

SEGISMUNDO:[*Aside*] If I am really dreaming, Heaven stop
Me from recalling, for so many things
Can't fall within the compass of one dream.
Oh, would to Heaven I could either know
How to escape them all, or not to think
Of any! Who has ever suffered grief
So hard to grasp? If I but dreamed about
That grandeur I experienced, how is
It that this woman can inform me now
Of facts that are well known to me? Then it
Was true, and not a dream; and if it was
The truth (which is another and no less
Confusing element), how can my life
Call it a dream? Are glories so akin
To dreams that real ones are considered false,
And false ones true? The difference is so slight
Between the two, there is some question as
To whether what we see and we enjoy
Is true or false! But is the copy so

Like the original that doubts arise
About which one it is? If that is true,
And all magnificence and majesty,
All pomp and power, are to disappear
Amid the shadows, let us learn to seize
This chance we get, for in reality
Alone we can enjoy what we enjoy
In dreams. Rosaura is within my grasp;
My heart adores her beauty; let us then
Enjoy this opportunity; desire
Suspends the laws of gallantry and trust
With which she hurls herself before my feet.
This is a dream, and since it is, let's dream
Our joys right now, for afterward they will
Be sorrows. But with my own reasons I
Convince myself again! If this is just
A dream, if this is but vainglory, who
Would sacrifice for human glory one
That is divine? What bygone bliss is not
A dream? Who has enjoyed great happiness
And does not say within himself, when he
Recalls it in his memory: "No doubt
I only dreamed all that I saw?" Well, then,
If this reveals my disillusionment,
If I know pleasure is a dazzling flame
That any passing breeze can change into
A heap of ashes, let us turn to the
Eternal, which is glory that endures,
Where neither happiness nor grandeur die.
Rosaura is without her honor, but

That is more fitting for a prince to give,
Not take away. By Heaven! I shall win
Her honor back before I gain my throne.
Her lure is strong; I must leave her alone.
[*To a soldier*] Sound out the call to arms! This day
                                        I fight
Ere shadows turn the gold of day to night!

ROSAURA: But sire! Dost thou take leave like this? Do not
My cares and anguish merit even one
Slight word from thee? How can it be, my lord,
That thou dost neither see nor hear me? Wilt
Thou not turn round at least and look at me?

SEGISMUNDO:Rosaura, it is vital to thy name
That to be noble to thee, I must now
Be cruel. If my voice does not respond
To thee, it is because my honor does;
Nor do I look at thee; in this hard case,
Thine honor must be watched, not thy fair face.
                [*Exit Segismundo, accompanied by soldiers*]

ROSAURA: Great Heavens! What enigmas are all these?
To think I must, after so many sighs,
Have doubts about equivocal replies!

SCENE ELEVEN

ROSAURA, CLARÍN.

CLARÍN: My lady, may I see thee now?
ROSAURA: Clarín!
Where hast thou been?
CLARÍN: I've been locked up, inside
A tower, reading fortunes in the cards

To see if I'm to be, or not to be.
And judging by the face-card I got first,
My life's at stake. I was about to burst.

ROSAURA: But why?

CLARÍN: Because I know the secret of
Just who thou art; indeed, Clotaldo is . . .
But what is all that noise? [*Drums are heard*]

ROSAURA: What can it be?

CLARÍN: It is a sally from the palace that's
Besieged, a squadron all equipped to fight
And conquer savage Segismundo's might.

ROSAURA: Then why am I a coward? Why not at
His side already, scandalizing all
The world, when now so much sheer cruelty
Is joined in battle's widespread anarchy? [*Exit*]

SCENE TWELVE

CLARÍN; *soldiers offstage.*

SOME VOICES: Long live our king!

OTHER VOICES: Long live our liberty!

CLARÍN: Let liberty and king both live for aye!
I do not care at all how I am cheered,
Provided I'm away, for I'll withdraw
Today in all this great confusion and
I'll play the rôle of Nero,[26] who did not
Show grief for anything. However, if
I want to grieve for something, it will be
For me. In hiding here, I'll see the show;

---

[26] Nero: *Roman emperor from 54 to 86 A.D. whose indifference during the burning of the city was traditional.*

*Clarin to
hide from Death*

This place among the rocks is safe and strong.
Since Death won't find me here, I'll catch my
                                                    breath,
And say that I don't care a fig for Death!
[*He hides; the sound of drums and clashing of arms offstage*]

SCENE THIRTEEN

BASILIO, CLOTALDO *and* ASTOLFO, *fleeing;* CLARÍN, *hidden.*

BASILIO: Is there a more unhappy king than I?
            Is there a father more beset with woes?

CLOTALDO: Thy vanquished army melts in mad retreat,
            Undisciplined and leaderless.

ASTOLFO: And now
            The traitors hold the field in victory.

BASILIO: In battles of this kind the winning side
            Consists of loyal forces: those who lose
            Are traitors. So, Clotaldo, let us flee
            My tyrant son's inhuman cruelty.
            [*Shots offstage; Clarín falls wounded from his
                                                hiding place.*]

CLARÍN: May Heaven help me!

ASTOLFO: Who is this poor man,
            This luckless soldier who has fallen here
            All bathed in blood?

CLARÍN: *He is shot*   I am a man who is
            Unfortunate, because in wanting to
            Protect myself from death, I found it here.
            In fleeing from it, I encountered it,
            Because there is no hiding place from death.
            Whence we conclude that he who flees it most

Turns out to be the one who finds it first.
Therefore, go back into the bloody fray
At once, for there amid the clash of arms
Lies greater safety than there is among
The most secluded hills; there is no course
That's safe against the force of destiny
Or unkind fate. No matter how you try
To free yourselves from death by fleeing it,
Remember you are sure to meet death still,
For you will die if it be Heaven's will.

[*He staggers off and falls.*]

BASILIO: Remember you are sure to meet death still,
For you will die if it be Heaven's will!
How well, oh Heaven, is our error and
Our ignorance corrected by this corpse
That speaks to us from out a gaping wound,
Whose gory eloquence reminds us that
Man's efforts are in vain when he arrays
Them all against divine omnipotence!
Yet I, to free my land from killings and
Sedition, placed it in the very hands
Of those from whom I sought to keep it free!

CLOTALDO: Although fate knows all bypaths, sire, and finds
The man it stalks among a tangled mass
Of mountain crags, it is not Christian-like
To say that there is no defense against
Its wrath. There is, indeed; a prudent man
Can be victorious over fate. If thou
Art not exempt from pain and sorrow, then
Do something to protect thyself from them.

ASTOLFO: Clotaldo, sire, addresses thee in words
            That match his wisdom and his riper years,
            But mine bespeak my boldness and my youth:
            Among the thickets of these hills there is
            A horse, swift beast begotten by the wind;
            Take flight, and meanwhile I shall guard the rear.

BASILIO: If Heaven's will is that I die, or if
            Grim Death expects to find me in this place,
            I'll meet him here and now, and face to face!
                    [*The call to arms is sounded.*]

                    SCENE FOURTEEN

    SEGISMUNDO, ESTRELLA, ROSAURA, *soldiers and retainers;*
            BASILIO, ASTOLFO, CLOTALDO.

SOLDIER: Amid these winding mountain trails, among
            These forest fastnesses, the king's concealed.

SEGISMUNDO: Pursue him! Have each tree upon this peak
            Examined trunk by trunk and branch by branch!

CLOTALDO: Please flee, my lord!

BASILIO: What for?

ASTOLFO: What dost thou have
            In mind to do?

BASILIO: Astolfo, stand aside!

CLOTALDO: What dost thou wish?

BASILIO: Clotaldo, I shall try
            The only remedy that's left to me.
                    [*He addresses Segismundo, and kneels.*]
            If thou dost come, young prince, in search of me,
            Behold me at thy feet, on bended knee.
            Make these white hairs thy rug upon the floor;

Step down upon my neck, and trample on
My kingly crown; disgrace, degrade, drag down
My reputation and my self-esteem;
Take vengeance on my honor, and make me
A captive slave. When all these deeds are through,
Thy will be done, oh Heav'n, thy word come true!

SEGISMUNDO: Illustrious Court of Poland, you who are
All witnesses to these amazing deeds,
Give ear to me: your Prince addresses you.
What Heaven hath decreed and God hath writ
With His own hand in characters of gold
Upon a field of blue, can never be
In error, never lie; the one who lies
And is in error is the one who tries
To penetrate and understand them to
Abuse them for some other purposes.
My father, who is here, to save himself
From my true nature's wrath, made me a brute,
A human beast; and so although, through my
High birth, my noble blood, and gallant strain,
I might have been both gentle and reserved,
This way of life and strange upbringing were
Enough to make my whole behavior wild:
A fine way to prevent my being so!
If it were said to any man, "Some wild
Inhuman beast will cause thy death," then would
It be a good idea to wake the beast
When it was sleeping? If they said, "This sword
That thou art wearing round thy waist will be
What kills thee," then in order to prevent

Its happening, it would be foolish to
Unsheathe the sword and place it at thy breast.
And if they said, "Wide waters are to be
The silver monument above thy tomb,"
Thou wouldst do wrong in putting out to sea
When it was raising whitecaps angrily
And curling crystal crests of snowy foam.
The same has happened to our King as to
The man who wakes the beast that threatens him,
The man who bares the sword he fears, the man
Who dares the stormy waves. And though my wrath
(Now heed me) were just like a sleeping beast,
My fury like a sword restrained, my rage
As quiet as a calm at sea, one's fate
Does not yield to injustice and revenge:
If anything, it is incited more.
And so, if one expects to overcome
His fate, it must be done with reason and
With moderation. Even one who sees
It coming cannot stave off harm before
It comes; although he can protect himself,
Of course, with humble resignation, he
Can only do this after the event,
Which in itself cannot be warded off.
May this extraordinary spectacle,
This most amazing scene, this horror, this
Phenomenon, be an example; there
Is nothing more surprising than to see,
Despite precautions of so many kinds,
A father prostrate at my feet, a king

Trod under foot. For it was Heaven's will;
No matter how he wanted to prevent
It, he could not. How then shall I, a man
Of younger years and not so brave as he,
Nor yet so learnèd, counter Heaven's will?
[*To the King*] Rise up, my lord, and let me clasp
                                                thy hand,

For now that Heaven has enlightened thee
About the error of thy ways in thine
Attempt to conquer it, my neck awaits
Thy vengeance humbly; I am at thy feet.

BASILIO: My son (for such a noble deed again
              Engenders thee as such within my heart),
              Thou art the Prince; the laurels and the palm
              Belong to thee, for thou hast conquered me;
              Now let thy deeds crown thee with victory.

ALL: Long live Segismundo! Long live he!

SEGISMUNDO: My sword must wait to gain great victories,
              So for today my greatest triumph is
              The victory I've won over myself.
              Astolfo, give thy hand in marriage to
              Rosaura right away; it is a debt
              Of honor, and I'll see that it is paid.

ASTOLFO: Although I owe her obligations, I
              Admit, take note that she does not know who
              She is, and it would be a stigma and
              Sheer infamy to wed a woman who . . .

CLOTALDO: Do not continue! Hold! Enough! Because
              Rosaura is as noble as thou art,

Astolfo, and my sword is ready to
Defend her on the field of honor; she
Is my own daughter, and that is enough!

ASTOLFO: What dost thou say?

CLOTALDO: I said that I, until
I saw her honorably married to
A nobleman, did not wish to reveal
Just who she was; her story is a long,
Involved one, but she is my child indeed.

ASTOLFO: Since that is so, I'll keep my plighted word.[27]

SEGISMUNDO: So that the fair Estrella will not be
Disconsolate about the loss of such
A valiant and outstanding prince, I shall
Myself hand-pick for her a husband who,
If he does not exceed Astolfo in
These merits and in fortune, is at least
His equal. Take my hand.

ESTRELLA: I do indeed
Gain much in winning such great happiness.

SEGISMUNDO: As for Clotaldo, who so loyally
Did serve my father, here my open arms
Await him, with what favors he may ask.

SOLDIER: If thus thou dost grant honors to one who
Has not served thee, then what of me, who caused
Revolt within the realm, the one who freed
Thee from the tower, what wilt thou give me?

SEGISMUNDO: The tower! And so thou wilt not escape
It ever, thou shalt stay in there until

---

[27] *While Astolfo's ideas seem contemptible to modern readers, in Calderón's day Astolfo could marry only a noblewoman.*

Thy death, close guarded; for the traitor is
Not needed when the need for treason's past.[28]

BASILIO: Thy wisdom is a marvel to us all.

ASTOLFO: And what a change his nature now reveals!

ROSAURA: And how discreet and prudent he's become!

SEGISMUNDO: What is it that surprises all of you?
What startles you, if my preceptor was
A dream, and in anxiety I fear
I shall awake and find myself again
Imprisoned? Even though this were not so,
It is sufficient just to dream it is.
For this is how I learned, so it would seem,
That all our mortal bliss fades like a dream.
And now I wish to use what time remains
To ask indulgence of such noble hearts,
And pardon for all errors in our parts.[29]

---

[28] *Imprisonment or death was the standard fate of traitors in Spanish plays, since it would have been unthinkable to allow treason to go unpunished.*

[29] *It was customary to close a play with a few lines of apology on the part of the actors.*